MW01114717

CHRONICLE

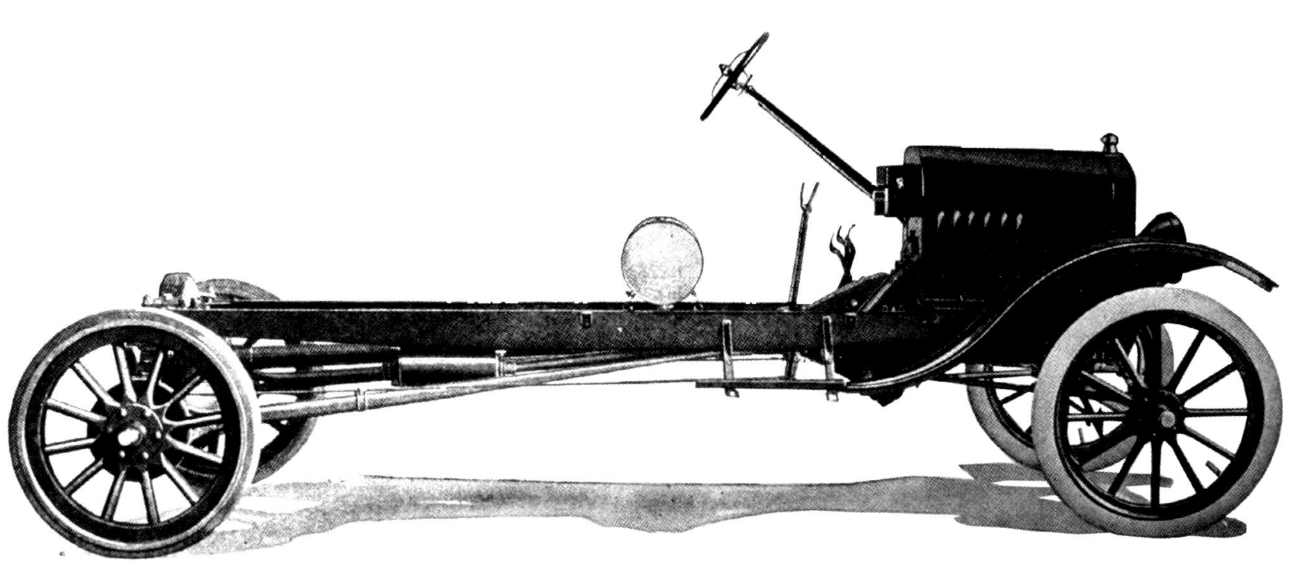

Publications International, Ltd.

Louis Weber, CEO
Publications International, Ltd.
7373 North Cicero Avenue
Lincolnwood, Illinois 60712

ISBN-13: 978-1-4127-1225-5
ISBN-10: 1-4127-1225-4

Manufactured in China.

8 7 6 5 4 3 2 1

The editors gratefully acknowledge those who supplied photography for this book:
Les Bidrawn, Jim Frenak, Thomas Glatch, Sam Griffith, Bud Juneau, Milton Kieft, Dan Lyons, Vince Manocchi, Doug Mitchel, Mike Mueller, Robert Nicholson, Nina Padgett-Russin, Gary D. Smith, David Temple, W.C. Waymack.

Special thanks to the owners of the trucks featured in this book:

1914: Carl. M. Riggins, 1914 Model T Depot Hack; Castle Amusement Park, 1914 Model T fire truck. **1930s**: Leroy J. Schaefer, 1930 Model A Roadster Deluxe pickup; Stephen Salazar, 1930 Sedan Delivery; Howard Bonner, 1930 Model AA dump truck; Sheldon Lake, 1931 Deluxe Delivery flower car; Leroy J. Schaefer, Model A pickup; Sheldon Lake, 1931 Town Delivery Car; Richard W. Andrews, 1931 Model A pickup; James R. Campbell, 1931 Postal Truck; Robert D. Brewer, 1931 Model A Deluxe Delivery; Arrowhead Water Co., 1931 Model AA water delivery truck; James Enders, 1934 pickup; Brad Boyajian, 1934 school bus; Donald F. Parker, 1934 Model BB Stake Bed; Dr. Edward and Joanne Dauer, 1934 BB gas truck; Dells Auto Museum/Dick and Lance Tarnutzer, 1936 Panel Delivery; G. Moyer and Connie Moyer, 1937 Sedan Delivery; Bill Henricks, 1937 pickup; Joe C. Schubert, 1938 pickup; Karl Benefiel, 1938 pickup; Dick Pyle, 1938 Panel Delivery; Mark Mendelsohn, 1938 COE Wrecker; John Roger Battistone, 1939 fire truck; William and Joseph Schoenbeck, 1939 pickup. **1940s**: Lloyd Duzell,1940 pickup; Robert N. Seiple, 1940 Sedan Delivery; Nelson D. Hansen, 1940 Panel Delivery; Nelson D. Hansen, 1940 Bell Telephone installer's truck; Robert Babcock, 1941 pickup; Ernest and Sheri Foster, 1942 pickup; Richard Tait, 1944 GPW (Jeep); Richard Staley, 1948 F-1 pickup; W.R. "Rick" Parsley, 1949 Panel Truck; Don Morris, 1949 F-1 Good Humor ice cream truck; Richard L. Youngman, 1949 F-1 pickup. **1950s**: Harry Fryer, 1950 F-1 pickup; Kenneth A. Coppolil, 1950 F-7 Howe fire truck; Jim Stewart, 1951 pickup; Michael Paris, 1951 F-1 Panel Delivery; Glen Bohannan, 1952 F-1 pickup; Dublin (Texas) Dr. Pepper, 1952 F-5; Jerry C. Spear and Christie A. Spear, 1954 F-100 pickup; Don Reeder, 1954 F-250 pickup; J. Talarico, 1955 F-100 pickup; Dale and Ana Callen, 1955 F-100 pickup; H.M. Martins, 1956 F-100 pickup; Tom Lerdahl, 1957 Ranchero; Ted Maupin, 1957 Courier Sedan Delivery; Richard Perez, 1958 F-100 pickup; Ted Maupin, 1958 Ranchero; Henry Alvarez/HSI Motors, Inc., 1959 Ranchero. **1960s**: Ken Anderson, 1960 F-100 Styleside pickup; Kenneth M. Hustvet, 1961 Econoline E-100 Custom Cab pickup; Jeff Blind, 1961 Econoline E-100 pickup; Ken M. Hustvet, 1961 Sedan Delivery; Mitchell Corporation of Owosso, 1961 A-1 Mutt; Ken M. Hustvet, 1961 Ranchero; Gary Wymore, 1963 Econoline E-100 pickup; Peter Stohbehn, 1963 Econoline E-100 pickup; Finn Fahey, 1965 F-100 Styleside pickup; Greg Ueatch, 1966 Bronco; Stephen and Teresa Shore, 1966 F-100 Custom Cab. **1970s**: Jim Reilly, 1970 Ranchero; A.W. Higginbotham, 1970 F-150; Brian Altizer, 1973 Bronco; Mike Hall, 1974 Bronco; Joe Bombaci, 1975 Bronco; Michell Garner, 1976 Bronco; Harold S. Boerschinger, 1977 Bronco; Steve Drake, 1979 Ranchero GT.

The editors also express their thanks for the generous assistance of Ford Motor Company.

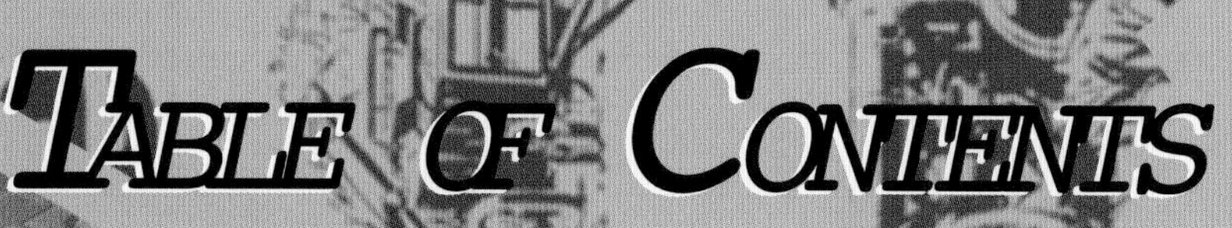

Table of Contents

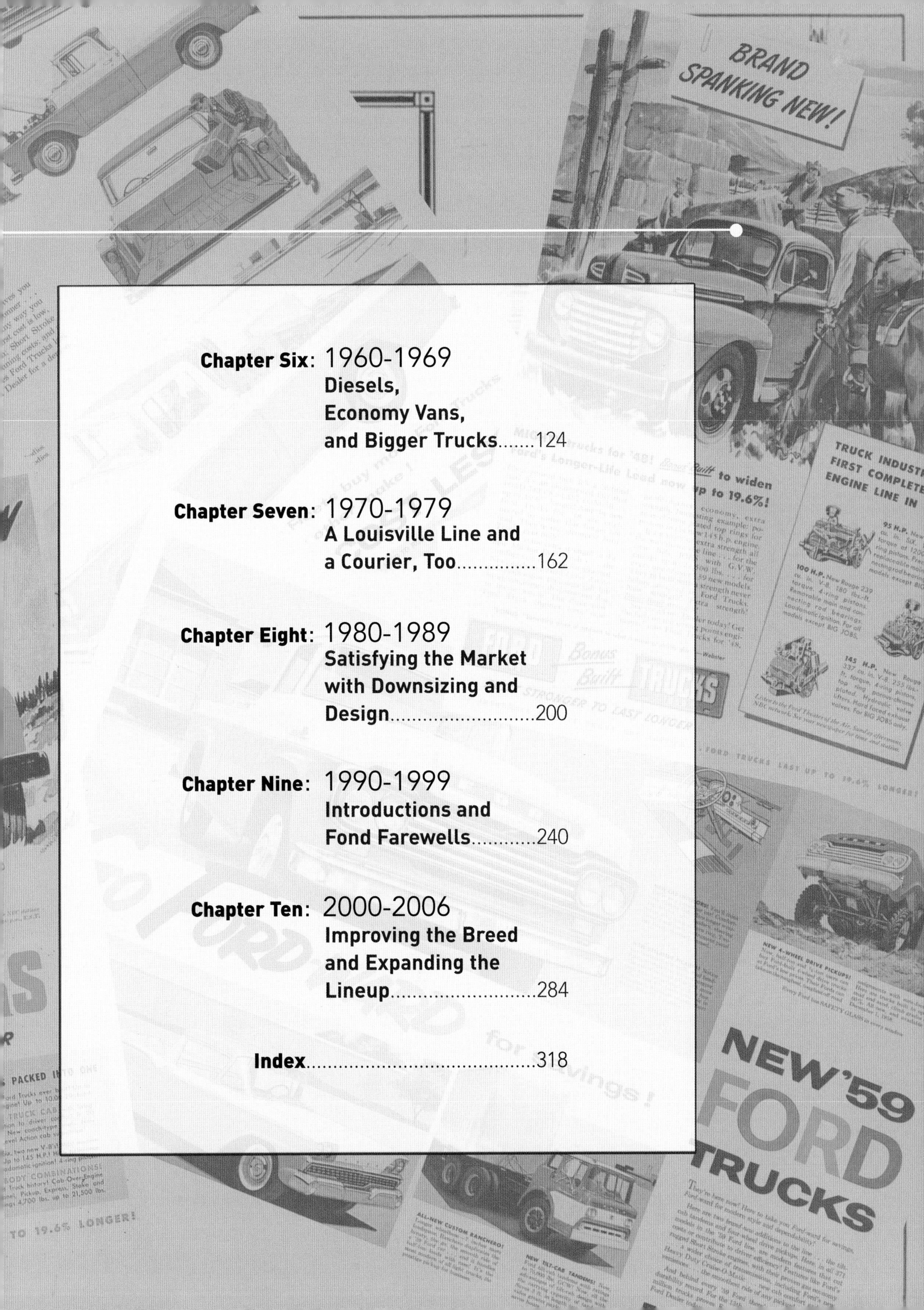
BRAND SPANKING NEW!
NEW '59 FORD TRUCKS

Ford Motor Company got its start in much the same manner as most other automobile manufacturers of the early 1900s: A mechanical genius joined forces with financial investors to build their own version of the American dream. What made Ford different from most others was innovation and wise management that has allowed the company to survive for more than 100 years.

A fledgling automobile industry already existed at the dawn of the 20th century, but these early "horseless carriages" were primarily the domain of the rich. Henry Ford changed all that with the Model T. But it wasn't just the car itself that brought personal transportation to the masses; it was a combination of good management, a solid sales organization, and the miracle of mass production.

While Ford Motor Company got its start building automobiles, an interest in commercial vehicles was evident almost from the beginning. Though early attempts at building trucks met with limited success, it was recognized that they were a useful commodity just waiting for the market to realize it.

The first of these trucks appeared in 1905, just two years after Ford's first automobiles. It was fitted with a boxlike cargo body behind the driver's seat, and while a useful conveyance, the Delivery Car was pulled from the market after just one year due to slow sales. A similar vehicle was introduced in 1912 on the Model T chassis, but it didn't exactly set the world afire, either.

By this time, various types of truck-type bodies were offered by outside suppliers for the Model T chassis, including everything from pickup beds to fire apparatus. But to most historians, the history of Ford trucks begins with the Model TT of 1917.

Though based on Model T mechanicals, the TT was a one-ton-rated truck. It carried unique features—such as a beefy frame, worm-gear differential, and solid-rubber rear tires—all aimed at providing a much higher payload capacity than the light-duty Model T chassis. It came only as a chassis with cab at first, with cargo bodies being supplied by outside companies; not until 1924 did Ford offer it with the Express body, essentially a pickup bed. Unlike previous commercial-vehicle attempts, it was a strong seller from day one.

Nineteen seventeen also brought another Ford workhorse: the Fordson tractor. Henry Ford had grown up on a farm and thus knew the rigors of the trade, and the Fordson was an attempt to do for rural areas what the Model T did for urban ones. And that it did; within months of going on sale, it became the best-selling tractor in the country. Because the Fordson contributed so much to the company's early success and often shared technology with its road-going brethren, these tractors have also been given exposure in *Ford Truck Chronicle*.

From there, Ford expanded into heavier-duty trucks: first the 1½-ton Model AA of 1928, then to bigger rigs that were rated at up to three tons by the late Forties. In the ensuing years, Ford expanded its lineup to include trucks in the highest weight classes, and all—from light-duty through medium-duty to heavy-duty—are covered within these pages.

Ford contributed mightily to the war effort during World War II, the company's vast resources being called upon to build a wide range of materiel used on land, sea, and air. Yet unlike some enterprises, Ford Motor Company did not emerge from the war on a strong financial footing. In fact, it was near collapse when Henry Ford II—the founder's grandson—took over, and, along with a wisely chosen cadre of associates, brought the company back.

One of the vehicles that helped the turnaround was Ford's first all-new postwar truck. Arriving for 1948—a year ahead of Ford's first new postwar car—it was a pickup that would go on to become a classic: the F-Series.

Initially called the F-1 in popular ½-ton form, the designation was changed in 1953 by adding "00" to the end of the model name. Thus the F-1 became the F-100, and this nomenclature continues to designate F-Series models to this day.

In the colorful history of the F-Series, two landmark years stand out, both quite unrecognized at the time. It was in 1978 that the F-150 began its unbroken streak as the nation's best-selling full-size pickup, and in 1983 that it began its continuous run as the nation's best-selling vehicle of *any* type.

Though it's the F-Series pickups for which Ford is probably best known, the company has built a wide variety of vehicles over the years that fall under the category of "trucks." Besides the aforementioned medium- and heavy-duty haulers, Ford has produced cargo-oriented Panel and Sedan Delivery wagons, the innovative car/pickup Ranchero, full-size passenger and cargo vans, and the currently popular crop of minivans and SUVs. All play an important role in Ford's long history, and all can be found in *Ford Truck Chronicle*.

The beginning of Ford's second hundred years has been marked by new challenges and a host of new products to meet them, a cycle that has been repeated many times in its history. If the past is any indication, Ford Motor Company will fight its way back and continue to fulfill the dream that started it more than a century ago. We don't think Henry would want it any other way.

—The Auto Editors of Consumer Guide®

Chapter One: 1903-1919
The Early Years

What would quickly become one of the world's largest automobile manufacturers got its start on June 16, 1903, when Henry Ford and his associates founded the Ford Motor Company. Production of the firm's first car, the two-cylinder Model A, began shortly thereafter, and was joined the following year by three new cars: the two-cylinder Model B and Model C, and the four-cylinder Model F. By the end of 1904, more than 2000 Fords had been built.

With sales of cars booming, Henry Ford had little reason to enter the commercial market, but he did make a few attempts to produce specialized vehicles during the early part of the century. The first example, based on a Model C Ford, was introduced in 1905. Called the Ford Delivery Car, its $950 price attracted few buyers, and less than a dozen were built before production ceased.

Ford's second attempt at a commercial

vehicle was called the Ford Delivery Van. Arriving in 1907, it was based on the four-cylinder Model N car introduced the previous year. Unfortunately, it only lasted about as long as its predecessor—and sold about as many copies.

Yet neither of these failures deterred Henry Ford from trying to establish a niche in the automotive world for his company and its products. And he would carve out more than just a niche with what would become one of the most famous and successful cars of all time: the Model T.

Introduced in October 1908 as a 1909 model, the venerable Model T was hardly revolutionary, being based heavily on the three-year-old Model N. But it struck a chord with buyers, its simple, reliable design being offered in a range of body styles with seating for two or five passengers. Furthermore, Ford dropped its previous four car lines to concentrate on the T, which allowed for increased production. And with that, Henry Ford was on his way to becoming an automotive icon.

1903-1919

Chapter One

But there was another event that took place in 1908 that would also make an indelible mark on the automotive landscape. That was when William C. Durant established General Motors, which would later become Ford's chief rival.

In 1910, Henry Ford transferred the production of his Model T from the Piquette Avenue plant in Detroit to a much larger facility in nearby Highland Park. Plants in Kansas City, Missouri; Long Island City, New York; and Minneapolis, Minnesota, would join it a few years hence.

Ford once again tackled the commercial end of the market in 1912 with two light-duty vehicles. One was the Commercial Roadster, which was basically a Model T Runabout with a removable rumble seat that could be replaced by an aftermarket-sourced commercial body. The other was the Model T Delivery Car. While more popular than Ford's previous two commercial vehicles, sales still weren't sufficient to convince Henry Ford to make a serious commitment to this market segment.

In 1913, the Model T became the first car to be built on a moving assembly line. This was a major advancement that greatly reduced the cost of manufacturing and helped Ford keep up with increasing demand. That year also saw the opening of plants in Chicago, Illinois, and Memphis, Tennessee.

In 1914, Ford initiated its $5 per day wage program, which was double the industry's normal rate of pay. This allowed Ford assembly-line workers to buy the cars they were building. It also helped to increase sales—which were growing by leaps and bounds anyway—prompting Ford to open another seven assembly plants.

Ford reached a major milestone in late 1915 with the production of its one-millionth vehicle. That year also saw the opening of nine new assembly plants, with another three added the following year. This rapid expansion in capacity would allow the company to build its two-millionth vehicle a scant 18 months later.

After watching his Model T cars being turned into trucks for several years, Henry Ford finally decided he wanted a piece of the action. So on July 27, 1917, he officially entered the truck business with the introduction of the one-ton-rated Model TT chassis. Now a customer could buy a stripped Model T chassis for light-duty commercial work or a heavier-duty Model TT version for bigger jobs. The year was also noteworthy for two other events: the introduction of the Fordson tractor, and the birth of Henry's first grandson, Henry Ford II. HFII, as he would later be known, was the son of Edsel, who had been born to Henry and his wife Clara in 1893.

During Ford's 1918 model year, Edsel Ford took over as president of the Ford Motor Company when his father relinquished that position, though there's little question Henry still exerted a lot of influence. Also during this time, some Ford plants were converted over to produce war materiel. Ford built a number of Model T ambulances for shipment to France, and opened a new plant to build submarine-chasing Eagle Boats.

The end of World War I on November 11, 1918, helped make 1919 a very good year for the Ford Motor Company. It brought the three-millionth Model T, along with the birth of Edsel's second son, Benson. It also saw construction start on the expansive Rouge River complex, which would eventually grow to become a nearly self-contained megafactory. Ford closed out the Teens as the country's undisputed sales leader, having produced nearly half of all vehicles sold in 1919.

1903-1913

1903: Ford Motor Co. founded; two-cylinder Model A starts at $850

1905: Delivery Car introduced—and then canceled

1906: Four-cylinder Model N starts at $600

1909: Model T introduced for $825

1910: Model T chassis goes on sale for $700; many chassis are used to make trucks

1912: Model T-based Delivery Car introduced

1913: Mass production begins; cars start at $525

1

1. Ford's first vehicle intended for cargo use was the Delivery Car, introduced in 1905. Based on a Model C chassis, only a handful were built before the body style was discontinued. The Delivery Car reappeared in similar form for 1912 on a Model T chassis, as shown here. 2. Station wagons would not be offered by Ford for some time, but forerunners such as this Depot Hack, so named because they ferried passengers to and from a train depot, were built by a number of outside suppliers. This one rides a 1914 Model T chassis.

2

1914: Ford stuns industry with $5/day wage; first year Model Ts offered only in black; new-car buyers get $50 rebate

1914

Model T chassis were adapted for all kinds of uses; this 1914 version was outfitted as a hook-and-ladder fire truck. During this era, Model Ts were powered by a 177-cubic-inch four-cylinder engine rated at a rousing 20 horsepower. The least-expensive "civilian" Model T, a two-passenger runabout, listed for $440, while a chassis (which included everything but the passenger compartment, trunk, and rear fenders) went for $410.

1915

1915: One-millionth Ford produced; prototype tractor shown

1. A farmer at heart, Henry Ford began experimenting with Model T-based tractors in the mid Teens. Because pulling a plow placed the engine under a constant heavy load, extra cooling capacity was needed; it was supplied by onc of the large cylindrical tanks beside the hood. The other held fuel. Frame rails that were normally straight were bent to allow for more ground clearance. 2. A 1915 photo shows one of Ford's experimental tractors next to a contemporary Model T.

1916: Nearly half of all cars built in U.S. are Fords; prices start at $345
1917: Painted steel radiators replace brass; U.S. enters World War I; first one-ton truck chassis offered; Fordson tractor goes on sale
1919: Electric starters and demountable rims offered on cars; prices rise, with cars starting at $500

A significant change to Model Ts occurred in 1917 when brass radiators gave way to painted steel ones. Like the rest of the vehicle, they came in any color the customer wanted—as long as the customer wanted black. 1. A Model T-based paddy wagon shows off an interesting type of tire used in the Teens. Though pneumatic tires were fitted to most cars by this time, many trucks had solid rubber tires on the rear to allow for higher load capacity. But these produced a brutally jolting ride, so some were "ventilated" with holes that went all the way through—from sidewall to sidewall—allowing the tread to flex a bit. Notice the rear tires are compressed somewhat at the bottom. 2. During World War I, which the U.S. entered in April 1917, Ford supplied thousands of ambulances for military use.

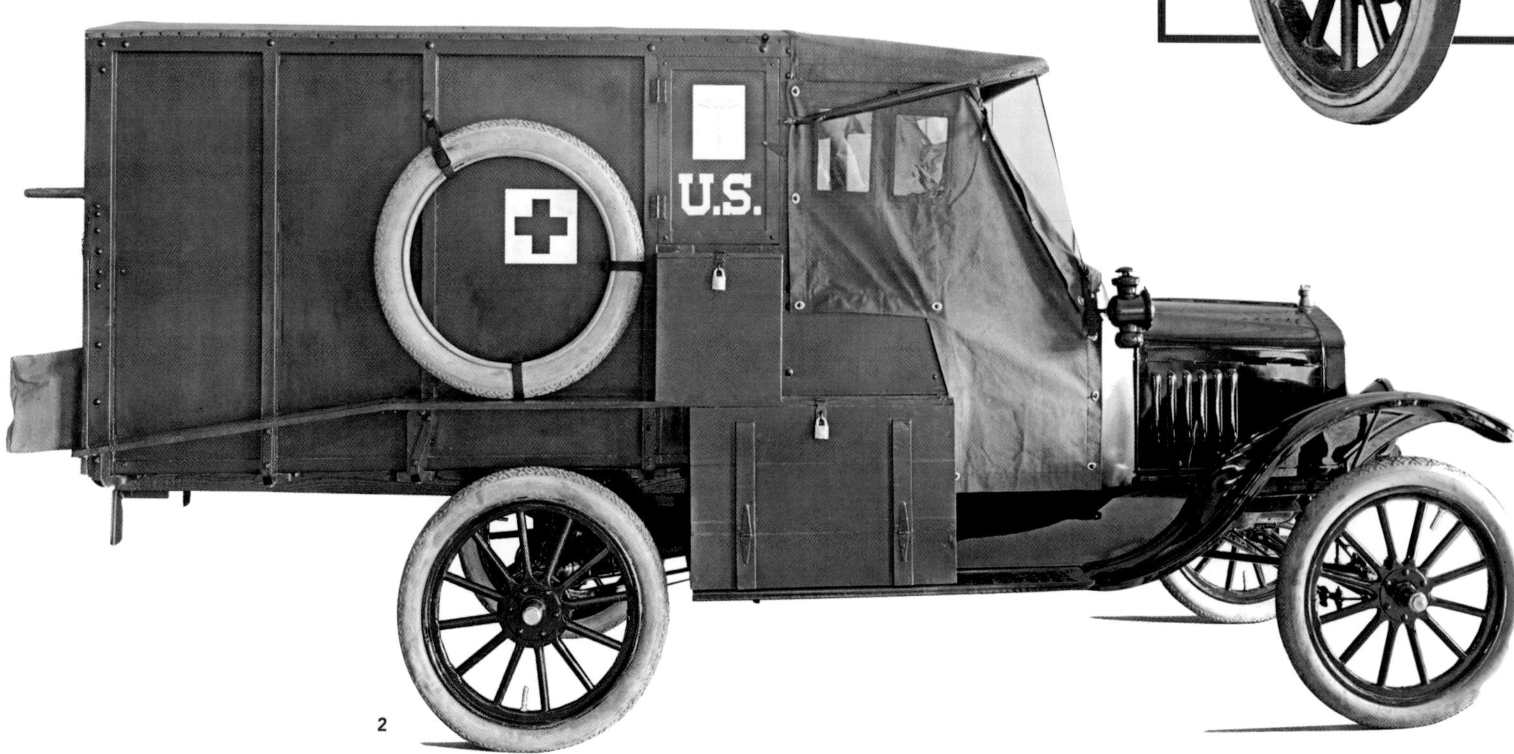

1. The first Ford chassis built expressly for truck duty arrived in 1917. Still based on Model T mechanicals but rated at one-ton capacity, it included a stronger frame and worm-gear differential along with solid rubber rear tires. 2. A one-ton truck chassis listed for $600 in 1918, significantly more than a standard Model T chassis, which sold for just $325. This example hosts a canopy-covered passenger compartment with weather protection, along with a stake-bed body. 3. Ford fitted this late-Teens Model T with a cargo box for the company's own use. A number of outside suppliers offered similar conversions. 4. A 1919 one-ton Ford chassis supports a fire-truck body—and seven firemen.

1

2

3

4

Chapter Two: 1920-1929

Ford Motor Company Grows with New Products and Acquisitions

Though Model Ts were becoming dated by the early Twenties, people continued to buy them in record numbers. One reason was that Henry Ford kept lowering their cost; from a starting price of $550 in 1920, one could be had for as little as $260 by 1925. But even low prices won't sell a product forever, and competitors were making inroads by offering features not available on the Model T.

Nevertheless, Ford car and truck production set new records during 1920, and Henry kept expanding facilities at the River Rouge Complex. Though these were positive points for the Ford Motor Company, not everything was rosy from a financial standpoint. Production was up, but sales were down by a substantial margin, which affected the amount of money coming into the company's coffers. As a result, Ford shut down its plants and shipped cars and trucks to dealers even though they had not ordered them. And those dealers had to pay for those vehicles on delivery and not when they were sold to customers. Dealers were not happy with this situation, but were forced to accept it if they wanted to maintain their Ford franchise.

1920-1929

Chapter Two

Nineteen twenty-one was a year of mixed results for the Ford Motor Company. In May the company celebrated the production of its five-millionth Model T, but this good news was offset by the defection of Ford's brilliant production boss, William Knudsen, to Chevrolet. It was largely due to this move that Chevrolet became an automotive juggernaut, passing Ford on the sales charts by the end of the decade.

Another bit of negative news that year was that Dodge Brothers, Inc., an up-and-coming rival, signed an agreement with the Graham Brothers Truck Company to become the sole distributor of that brand. Later in the decade, Dodge would absorb Graham to become another serious competitor to Ford.

Things looked a little better for the Ford Motor Company in 1922. A new blast furnace was dedicated at the River Rouge Complex, and production of the Fordson tractor at this facility set a new record. Henry Ford also expanded his company's holdings by purchasing the assets of the Lincoln Motor Company for $8 million. For 1923, Ford updated the look of the Model T cars and Model TT trucks, and total production of these vehicles topped 1.8 million units for the year.

Prior to 1924, Henry Ford sold his Model TT trucks as rolling chassis, leaving the body business to aftermarket companies. This attitude changed that year when Ford's first factory-catalogued truck was offered as the Model TT with Express (pickup) Body. The following year brought a lighter-duty version based on the car chassis. Called the Model T Runabout with Pickup Body, it sold for the modest price of $281. Also during 1925, Ford opened its first plant in Mexico, built its 12-millionth vehicle, and set a new truck production record of more than 270,000 units. And William

Clay Ford, Henry's third grandson, was born.

In order to stimulate sales of the decidedly old-fashioned Model T, 1926 brought an option to Henry's famous "Any color as long as it's black" dictum that originated in 1914, with available hues of grey, green, and maroon. But the writing was on the wall. The Model T had outlived its usefulness, and shortly after building the 15-millionth copy in May 1927, production finally ground to a halt.

The shutdown, however, was only temporary; Ford had an all-new design waiting in the wings. And what rolled out of plants later that year would make contemporary buyers forget all about the old "Tin Lizzie."

That new Ford, called the Model A, was introduced to the public on December 2, 1927. It was followed shortly thereafter by the Model AA trucks, and both were a hit with buyers.

More stylish than the Model Ts and TTs they replaced, the new cars and trucks came with more standard equipment, a more powerful engine, and an easier-to-use transmission. So advanced and price-competitive were these vehicles that they became the hit of the 1928 model year.

Ford trumped the industry again in 1929 when it introduced a new factory-built light-duty model: the wood-bodied Station Wagon. But few events—automotive or otherwise—could match what was about to take place. For on October 29, thereafter referred to as "Black Tuesday," the nation's financial well-being would be dealt a serious blow as the stock market began to crash, triggering the Great Depression.

1920

1920: Lincoln, which would later become part of Ford Motor Co., begins production

1921: William S. Knudsen leaves Ford for rival Chevrolet; 5-millionth Model T built; Dodge Brothers begin distributing Graham Brothers trucks, soon to be staunch competitors of Ford

1922: Model T production tops 1.1 million for the model year; Ford purchases Lincoln

1923: Ford institutes Weekly Purchase Plan, a pay-as-you-drive program that allows more people to buy a Model T

1

2

1. Oakland, California-based Dreyer's trusted this 1920 Ford Model T truck to deliver ice cream to stores. Both companies are still in business.
2. This Model T was converted into a truck, which in turn was converted into a snowmobile. The fenders were probably removed to accommodate the second rear axle, which allowed use of tanklike treads.

Advertising..............

One of Ford's 1923 ads carried a simple message: A Ford cost less to buy and drive than virtually any other car, and businesses would do well to adopt them. Since Ford's sales and profits soared during this period, perhaps the advertising did its job, but it's hard to imagine such a dour-faced spokesman being used today.

A 1920 Depot Hack is fitted with the demountable rims that became available on a broader range of vehicles that year. The rims allowed for easier flat repair, as the outer rim—which held the tire—could be separated from the wheel hub, which remained on the vehicle.

1. Crowds turn out to view a lineup of Fordson tractors in 1926, two years before the end of production. Even at this time, horses were still the primary source of power on most small farms.
2. Henry Ford (left) with his only son, Edsel, in front of an early Fordson tractor. Whether Edsel influenced the naming of the tractor (being "Ford's son") is unclear, but after Edsel's untimely death in 1943, he most certainly influenced the name of the ill-fated Edsel car of the late 1950s.

Tractors

Henry Ford appreciated the hard life farmers endured, and introduced the Fordson tractor in 1917 in an effort to mechanize the nation's farms.

Though "Ford" would seem to be the more logical moniker, that name was already taken. A company in South Dakota had hired a man named Ford, ostensibly a tractor engineer (which he wasn't), so it could rightfully use his name on its tractors; an obvious—though legal—way to capitalize on Henry's reputation.

Henry countered by using the name "Fordson" on his machines. Being small, light, and inexpensive, they were immediately popular, quickly becoming the nation's best-selling tractor. As with the Model T, Henry dropped the Fordson's price over the years, prompting competitors to do the same. This brought the cost of all tractors down to where more farmers could afford one, thus helping Henry achieve his goal.

1. A Fordson fitted with crawler tracks and wooden skis hauls an impressive load of logs through the snow—probably very slowly. 2. In this 1930s photo, an early Fordson and a Model T truck share a farmer's admiration.

Tractors

1. A 1925 Fordson display shows off both the tractors and the implements they could pull. 2. Fordson ads from the mid Twenties stressed the advantages of a tractor to farmers still using horses. 3. A threshing machine is driven off the pulley of a Fordson via a long leather belt. Early tractors were as often used for powering equipment as for pulling plows.

To Make Farming More Profitable

Fordson

To make farming more profitable—to make the farmer's life and the lives of his family happier and more abundant, is the aim of the Ford Motor Company in manufacturing the Fordson Tractor.

For by helping him to get more work done in less time and at less cost than formerly, the Fordson Tractor lightens the farmer's burden.

The vast resources of the Ford organization and the highly scientific factory methods which produce them so economically in such large numbers, and of such splendid quality, make possible the low cost price of Fordson Tractors and their superb performance.

Nowhere can the American farmer secure for so little a Tractor that will accomplish so much. The Fordson Tractor is a practical, time-saving aid in plowing, harrowing, planting, mowing, harvesting, threshing, road-mending and scraping, timber-cutting and sawing, hauling, pumping, excavating—in fact every duty the farmer must perform which requires power.

Ask your Fordson Dealer, or write us, for an actual demonstration, on your farm, of what the Fordson can do for you.

Ford Motor Company
Detroit, Michigan

2

1

3

1924

1. Ford's first truck cab, called (appropriately) the Open Cab, appeared in 1924, featuring a slanted windshield and C-shaped side openings. It's fitted here to a Model TT one-ton chassis.
2. For light-duty use, a Model T chassis was still available. Note the oval-shaped fuel tank that was fitted to Model Ts beginning in the early 1920s.
3. A Model TT with Open Cab hosts a new-for-1924 Express Body pickup bed—Ford's first truck bed. This example is fitted with canopy top, screens, and side curtains. 4. A similar canopy top covers the wood-panel body of this Model T passenger vehicle. The side-mounted spare tire is fitted to a demountable rim. 5. A 1924 Model T with panel body shows off that year's styling changes, which included a taller radiator and hood. It was owned by the Pioneer Tea Co. of Detroit.

1925

1924: Ford offers first truck body, an express pickup bed, which soon gets optional canopy and side curtains; Model Ts updated with taller radiator and hood

1925: Closed truck cabs introduced; first real "pickup" debuts, a Model T Runabout with pickup body; 12-millionth Ford built; one-millionth Ford truck built; 500,000th Fordson tractor built

1. Ford's first real pickup was introduced for 1925: a Model T Runabout with pickup body. This example is shown carrying a weighty load of bananas. 2. A Model T coupe is fitted with a large box trunk, perfect for delivering small items. 3. A floral shop made deliveries with a sliding-door body on a 1925 Model T chassis. 4. In a "radical" restyle for 1926, Model Ts got a taller hood that flowed straight into the cowl, as shown on this Runabout pickup.

1

1926-1927

1926: Model Ts get taller radiator and hood, both situated at cowl height; newly available on Ts are a nickeled radiator and, for the first time since 1913, body colors other than black; Model TT trucks retain old design

1927: In overall sales—both car and truck—Ford is surpassed by rival Chevrolet as little-changed Model T falls out of favor; after more than 15 million were built, Model T production ends in spring 1927, prompting many Ford plants to temporarily shut down

1. Despite the fact Ford now offered its own truck bodies, outside manufacturers continued to sell special-purpose varieties, such as this panel delivery fitted to a 1926 Model T chassis. 2. Though the colors are difficult to differentiate in this black-and-white photograph, this 1927 Model T Runabout pickup shows off the newly available two-tone color scheme, which always left the fenders and running boards in black. It proved to be among the last Model Ts made, as production ceased in spring 1927, after more than 15 million had been built.

1

1928-1929

1928: Model T car and Model TT truck replaced by Model A and AA, respectively; Model AA rated at 1 1/2 tons vs. one ton for TT; old 177-cubic-inch four-cylinder engine gives way to new 200-cid four with more-modern technology and twice the horsepower, now 40; three-speed sliding-gear transmission replaces two-speed planetary gearbox; four-wheel brakes adopted

1929: Ford returns to number one in sales as production of the Model B reaches full capacity; Model BB trucks gain disc wheels, bigger brakes, and a four-speed gearbox late in the model year; stock market crashes on October 29, 1929, prompting the Great Depression

2

1. Ford replaced the venerable Model T in 1928 with the completely new Model A. Like its predecessor, the A formed the basis for a truck chassis, the AA, which was rated at 1 ½ tons vs. 1 ton for the Model TT. The company's first panel-truck bodies also arrived that year and could be fitted to either the A or AA chassis; it's shown here on the former. 2. Among the Model A truck offerings was this closed-cab pickup. Both the A and AA carried a 200-cubic-inch four-cylinder engine producing 40 horsepower—twice that of the Model T's 177-cid four—along with a sliding-gear three-speed transmission.

3

4

3. As might be expected, the 1929 Model B changed little after its ´28 redesign—and it didn't need to; for the first time in three years, Ford topped Chevrolet in sales. This closed-cab pickup sold for $475. 4. For about $30 less, buyers could get a Model A pickup with an open cab.

Chapter Three: 1930-1939

Ford Fights the Depression with Better Cars for Less Money

The Thirties dawned in a dismal state as the Great Depression took hold. People were out of work, standing in breadlines, and money to buy anything—let alone new cars and trucks—was scarce. Profits made during the Roaring Twenties seemed to disappear overnight, and many automakers didn't weather the financial storm.

Ford managed to survive, of course, partly due to its sheer size and depth of resources. But the company helped its own cause by not resting on its laurels, instead bringing out better-looking, better-performing vehicles offered in a greater variety of models. And steady price cuts didn't hurt, either.

Styling changes to the 1930 and '31 Model A cars and Model AA trucks made them look fresh, and several special models were added to widen the make's appeal. But this turned out to be just a warm-up for what was soon to come.

During these years, chief rival Chevrolet offered a six-cylinder engine, which was considered a competitive advantage over the four-cylinder found in the Model A. So when Henry Ford began brainstorming a successor to the A, he decided to trump Chevrolet with a V-8 engine.

1930-1939

Chapter Three

When it was introduced in March 1932, the V-8-powered Model 18 was a sensation right out of the gate. A four-cylinder version, called the Model B, was also offered, since it was felt many people would be attracted to its greater economy—and lower price. But so popular was the V-8 that the four-cylinder would quickly fade from the scene.

The problem with introducing a car in 1932 was that this was the worst year of the Great Depression. Not many people were interested in buying a new Ford, V-8 engine or no. Yet the powerplant gave the low-priced car an upmarket feature not offered by rivals, which undoubtedly helped sales.

Ford had originally planned for the V-8 to be used in cars only, not in trucks—odd, since it would seem to be a natural for heavy-duty haulers. But this plan quickly changed when truck buyers began clamoring for the new engine.

Nineteen thirty-three was a big year for Ford milestones. The company celebrated its 30th anniversary, along with the production of its 21-millionth vehicle. Ford was also a major participant in the "Century of Progress" exposition held in Chicago that year, and Henry Ford proudly opened his Greenfield Village complex in Dearborn. This multifaceted display was his salute to American history and the American way of life in its earlier days.

Due to low demand, 1934 was the last year not only for the four-cylinder engine, but also for open-cab trucks. Since both of these represented the least-expensive alternatives, it was a subtle signal that the economy was finally beginning to improve.

Further proof came in 1935, which turned out to be a great year for Ford. Both the cars and trucks featured engineering improvements and new styling, and customers responded. When the tally was counted at the end of the year, more buyers chose Fords—both cars and trucks—than any other make.

Despite the success of the V-8, Ford was sometimes criticized for not offering an "economy" engine. So in 1937, the company responded by adding a radically downsized V-8. Whereas the original (which continued) displaced 221 cubic inches and produced 85 horsepower, the new V-8 was sized at just 136 cid with a rating of 60 hp. While the difference in power between the two didn't look like much on paper, in reality, the smaller engine was just too small, and like the four-cylinder that preceded it, was soon dropped.

Ford also entered the transit-bus business in 1937 with the introduction of the forward-control chassis, which placed the engine off to one side so the driver could sit next to it rather than behind it. The company also began offering trucks in fancier Deluxe trim.

Both 1938 and 1939 were significant years for Ford cars and trucks. Ford's pickups were fitted with a new cab, front-end sheetmetal, and bed for 1938, while 1 ½-ton versions got a new chassis. A further attraction was the debut of a truck that slotted between the light-duty car-based pickup and the heavy-duty 1 ½-ton models. Rated at one ton, the new series was appropriately called the "One-Tonner." It would be followed by a Three-Quarter Tonner the following year. Also introduced by Ford in 1938 were the industry's first Cab-Over-Engine (COE) models.

While the big news of 1939 was the beginning of World War II, which would have a profound effect on people around the globe, the big news at Ford Motor Company was the introduction of the Mercury. Aimed at cars like Pontiac, Oldsmobile, Hudson, and Dodge, it gave Ford a competitor in the midpriced field. It also brought a larger V-8 engine of 239 cid and 95 hp, which would quickly find its way into Ford trucks.

Nineteen thirty-nine will also be remembered as the year Henry Ford finally buckled to buyer pressure and replaced his vehicles' old-fashioned mechanically actuated brakes with modern hydraulic units. Virtually all Ford's competitors had made the switch years before, and though Henry didn't trust the new systems, their absence on Ford vehicles was considered a safety detriment.

To close out this decade, it should be mentioned that Canada joined Great Britain in late 1939 by declaring war on Germany, and soon thereafter, the Ford Motor Company of Canada, Ltd., started producing military specification vehicles for the war effort. It was an omen of things to come for the parent company, as the United States would enter the war two years later.

1930

1930: Revised styling gives sleeker look; AA trucks offer longer chassis; Depression sours sales; Fordson tractor returns after two-year hiatus

1931: Ford drops to number two in sales behind Chevrolet; truck-body offerings expand to include several low-volume styles, many still built by aftermarket companies but offered through Ford dealers

1. First offered on trucks for 1930, Deluxe trim included stainless-steel radiator and headlights, which really helped dress up this Vermillion Red pickup. Broad whitewalls and a chromed spare-tire cover didn't hurt either. Regardless of body color, the fenders—which trailed back farther in front for 1930—were always black. 2. A restored Deluxe-trim Sedan Delivery shows off the side-hinged rear door that provided easy access to cargo. 3. A similar vehicle was used by the Eagle Baking Company of Brooklyn, NY. 4. Wood-bodied station wagons could seat up to eight passengers.

A rare 1930 AA dump truck on the standard 131 ½-inch wheelbase shows off the steel disc wheels adopted by heavy-duty Ford trucks during the 1929 model year, as well as the available dual rear wheels. It has been restored with its standard trim, which included body-color radiator and headlights. Power comes from a 200-cubic-inch, 40-horsepower four-cylinder engine similar to that used in contemporary Model A cars, but it's mated to a four-speed transmission (vs. a three-speed) for a wider range of gear ratios.

1930

1-2. An unusual truck based on the Model A (103 ½-inch wheelbase) chassis was the Deluxe Pickup, featuring a high-walled cargo bed integral with the cab. Chrome rails were fitted to the top of its wood-lined bed. Many were used by General Electric to promote refrigerator sales, but the body style would be discontinued after 1931. 3. A Deluxe-trim Model A pickup with standard cargo bed features a canopy, under which produce was often sold.

4. Among the multitude of low-production body styles Ford offered during the Depression was this elegant Town Car Delivery. Introduced for 1930, this '31 model displays the sloped windshield it gained that year. It came with carriage lamps and bright-metal spare-tire cover, and could be fitted with a canopy over the driver's area. The cargo compartment was formed from aluminum and lined with wood paneling. This distinctive body style would disappear after 1931.

1931

A Deluxe-trim Model A pickup was a Depression-era beauty. This 1931 model displays the new pickup box introduced that year, which replaced a design that had been in use since 1925. At 59.4 × 46 ×16.7 inches, the box was about three inches longer, six inches wider, and nearly four inches taller than the older version.

1. A restored 1931 Model A postal truck carries its original California license number. Note the sliding side door, which has been left open. 2. Mounted on the 131½-inch AA chassis and based on the convex-roofed Deluxe Panel body was the Funeral Service Car. It can be identified by its wide side window. 3. The same chassis is shown holding an Express pick-up body with optional canopy.

1931

1

2

3

1. This 1931 Ford Model A Deluxe Delivery was restored to resemble a New Era Dairy truck the owner's father had driven in Herrin, Illinois, after World War II. 2-3. A standard AA chassis holds short and tall versions of a Stake Body, popular for hauling freight. 4. This restored 1931 Model AA carries the weight of 72 five-gallon glass bottles. It's mounted on the longer wheelbase (157 inch) AA chassis that joined the standard 131 ½-inch AA chassis for 1930. The long-wheelbase version could carry bodies up to 12 feet in length; previously, the standard chassis required aftermarket frame extensions for bodies over nine feet. 5. Another special offering by Ford during the early Thirties was this Combined Dump and Coal Body, which had sides that were taller than those of standard dump bodies.

4

5

1932

1932: Flathead V-8 introduced as an option to the four-cylinder; cars and trucks get "rounded-edge" grilles covering their radiators; "Model B" denotes four-cylinder line, "Model 18" the V-8s; sleeker design sits on longer, 106-inch wheelbase; Model B pickup bed extended more than 10 inches to 69.7; Depression bottoms out

1

2

1. At about 800 Depression-era dollars, the Station Wagon was an expensive proposition when a Fordor sedan started at $540, but the wagon seated eight vs. five for the sedan. 2. Star of the 1932 line was Ford's new flathead V-8. Displacing 221 cubic inches and producing 65 horsepower, it was offered alongside an improved four-cylinder, now rated at 50 hp. 3. Thanks in part to a wheelbase stretched nearly 3 inches to 106, Model B pickup beds grew more than 10 inches in length for 1932 to nearly 70 inches. Shown is a prototype of the Open Cab Pickup, of which few were built.

1933

1933: Ford cars get radically new streamlined styling, but only the Station Wagon and Sedan Delivery follow suit on the truck side as other styles carry over 1932 lines

Compare this 1933 BB Stake truck to the similar 1931 model shown a couple of pages back. Note this vehicle's rounded-off grille and arched headlight bar, along with its rear leaf springs that are inverted and centered over the axle in what we'd now call "normal" fashion.

1934

1934: V-8 boosted to 85 horsepower for cars, somewhat less for lower-compression trucks; four-cylinder fades away, as does the Open Cab

1-3. Trucks didn't share the car line's sleek 1933 styling alterations, but did get a thicker grille housing and lower headlight bar, as shown on this little-changed '34 pickup. Ford's V-8 had grown so popular that the four-cylinder engine was fazed out during the model year, as was the roadsterlike Open Cab body for trucks. 4. Model BB chassis saw varied uses, as evidenced by this 1934 school bus.

STOP
SCHOOL BUS
STOP
SCHOOL BUS
No 1
GOLDEN BEAR TRANSIT
GB
4

1934

1. Carrying its original oak Stake Bed is a V-8-powered 1934 Model BB on the standard 131 ½-inch-wheelbase chassis. 2. The longer 157-inch chassis hosted this Texaco tanker. A full load of fuel doubled its 7500-lb curb weight.

1935-36

1935: Trucks finally treated to a facelift that is similar though not identical—to what Ford cars got in '33

1936: Few changes to either the car or truck line

1. As before, the 1936 Sedan Delivery was based on the car line, and thus carried the fuller fenders and tapered headlight housings of Ford's passenger vehicles. A side-hinged rear door gave easy access to cargo.

2. A 1935 redesign for the truck line brought a more curvaceous grille, skirted fenders, and laid-back windshield, which left them closer in appearance to contemporary Ford cars. A little-changed 1936 pickup is shown. Note the difference in fender contour compared to that of the Sedan Delivery above.

1

2

1936

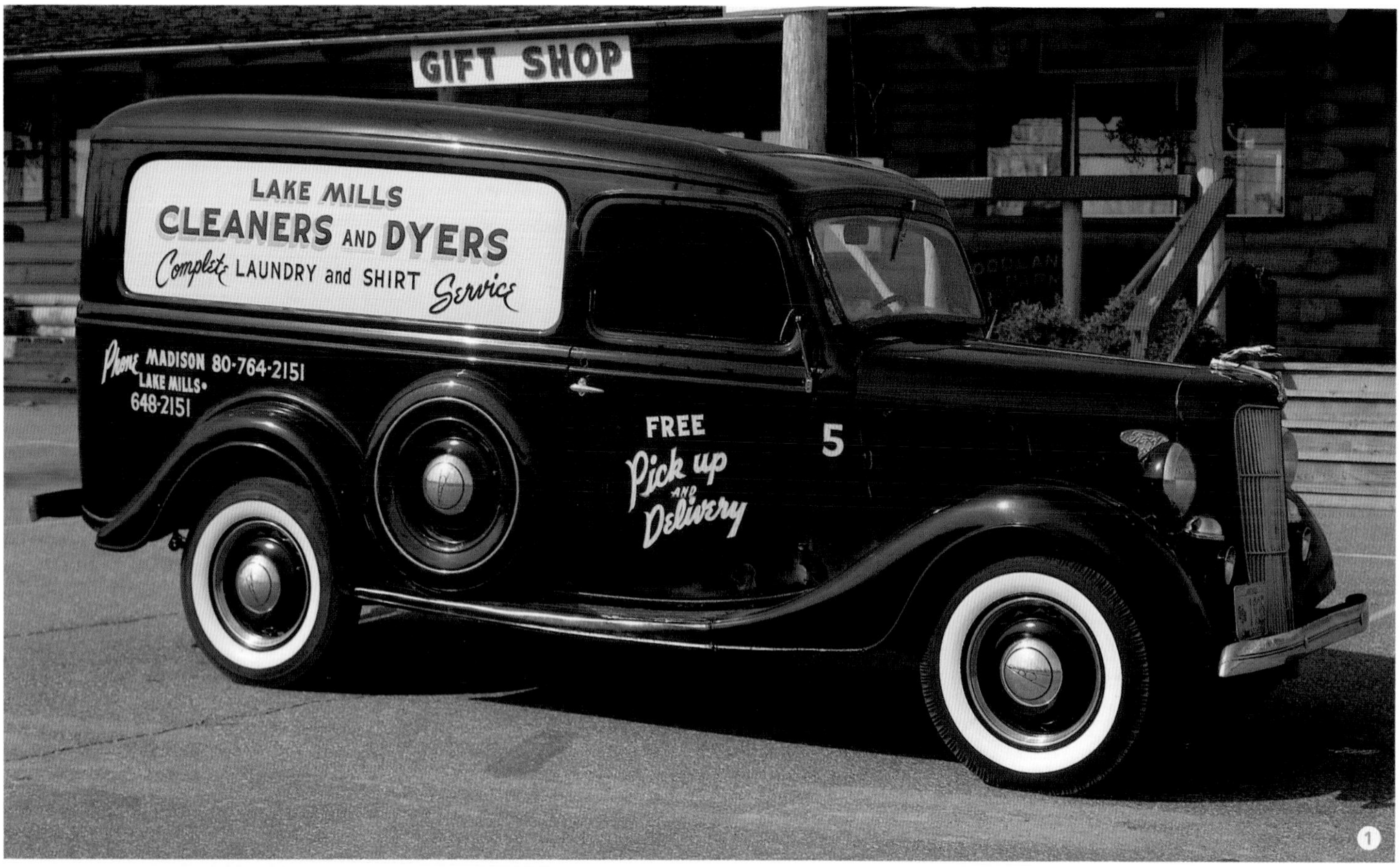
GIFT SHOP
LAKE MILLS
CLEANERS AND DYERS
Complete LAUNDRY and SHIRT Service
Phone MADISON 80-764-2151
LAKE MILLS•
648-2151
FREE
Pick up and Delivery
5

1

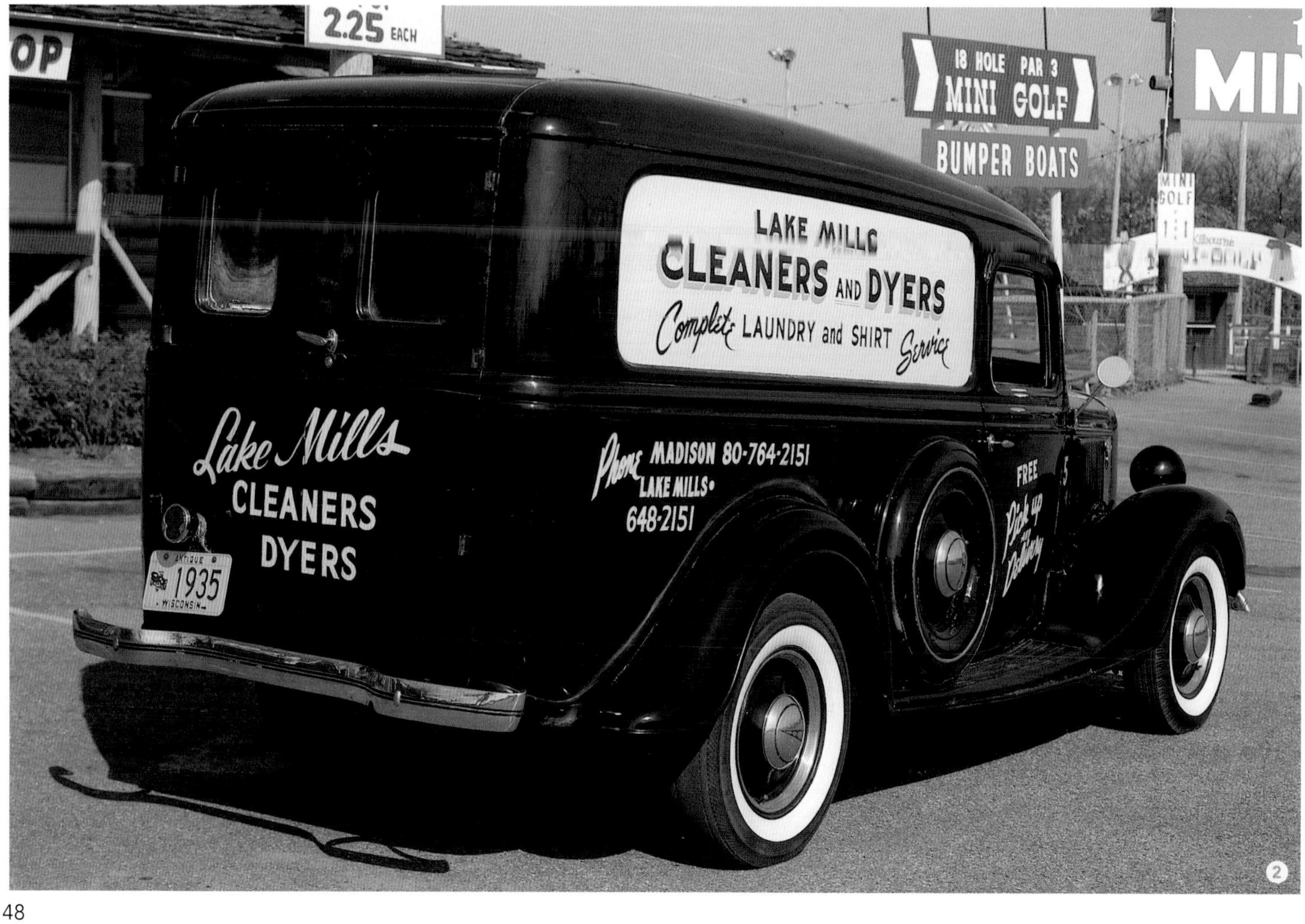
2.25 EACH
18 HOLE PAR 3
MINI GOLF
BUMPER BOATS
LAKE MILLS
CLEANERS AND DYERS
Complete LAUNDRY and SHIRT Service
Lake Mills
CLEANERS
DYERS
Phone MADISON 80-764-2151
LAKE MILLS•
648-2151
FREE
Pick up and Delivery
ANTIQUE
1935
WISCONSIN

2

1937

1937: Cars get a radical facelift, trucks a milder one; smaller 136-cubic-inch 60-horsepower flathead V-8 joins the larger, 85-hp version; Ford trucks regain first place in sales race

1-2. Unlike the Sedan Delivery, the Panel Delivery was truck based, so it carried truck styling—along with dual side-hinged rear doors, a larger cargo compartment, and higher payload capacity. This ´36 model is nearly identical to the redesigned ´35. The chrome grille identifies it as a Deluxe version. 3-4. New styling that placed the headlights partially into the fenders graced the 1937 car line, as shown on this Sedan Delivery. Harder to see is its split, vee'd windshield, another ´37 innovation. It also carries the newly available rear-mounted spare tire that opened up space in the cargo compartment.

1937

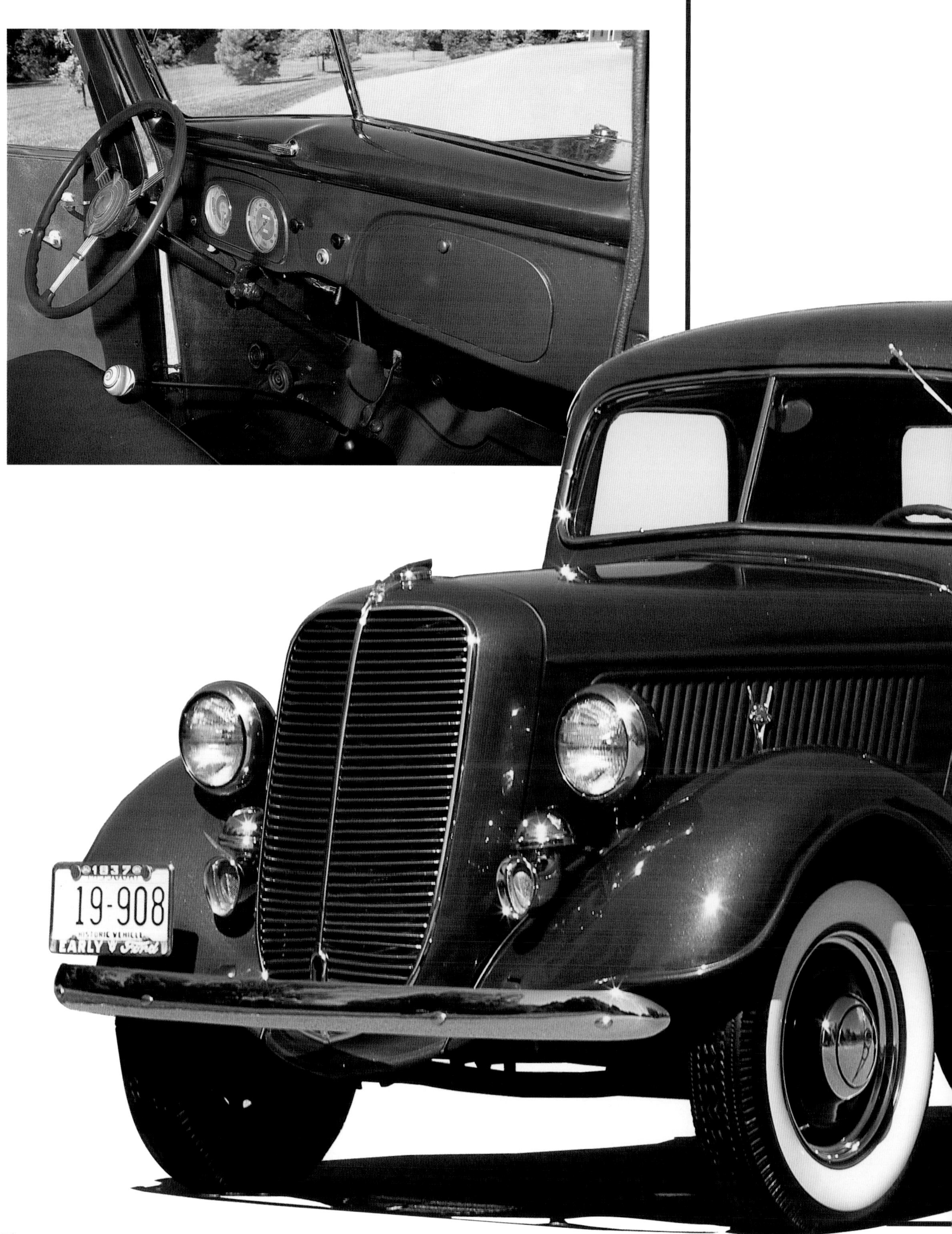

Trucks got a fuller grille and vee'd windshield for '37, but didn't look anywhere near as modern as the car line. All pickups had a V-8—along with the appropriate badge on the side of the hood—but newly offered that year was a 136-cubic-inch 60-horsepower version that promised better fuel economy than its bigger 221-cid 85-hp brother.

1938

1938: Car line adopts two different styling themes, with Standard models carrying over ´37 traits, while Deluxe versions get more modern look; trucks get fuller fenders, oval grille, new cab, and revised pickup bed; One-Tonner model added to truck line to bridge gap between car-based models and 1 ½-ton truck models; 131 ½-inch truck chassis extended to 134 inches, while 157-incher remains; Ford introduces new line of Cab-Over-Engine trucks; recession hits industry as Chevrolet takes lead in truck sales—which it would hold for 30 years

1-4. Bulbous front and rear fenders along with an oval grille marked the 1938 Ford pickup trucks, which also got a new cab and pickup bed.

1938

1-3. As before, the Panel Delivery carried truck styling, but got a new body for 1938. 4-5. A wrecker sports the Cab-Over-Engine (COE) chassis and body Ford introduced for 1938. It provided for a shorter overall length with a given-size utility body—which in this case was pretty short to begin with. 6. This 1938 fire truck was used by Ford at its Rouge Plant in Detroit.

ASSAY OFFICE
GRUBSTAKE MINE CO.
LOCAL HONEY
BARLOW
Towing

4

UNION
ICE
ASSAY OFFICE
GRUBSTAKE MINE CO.
1938
BARLOW
Towing
A Ford able Service

5

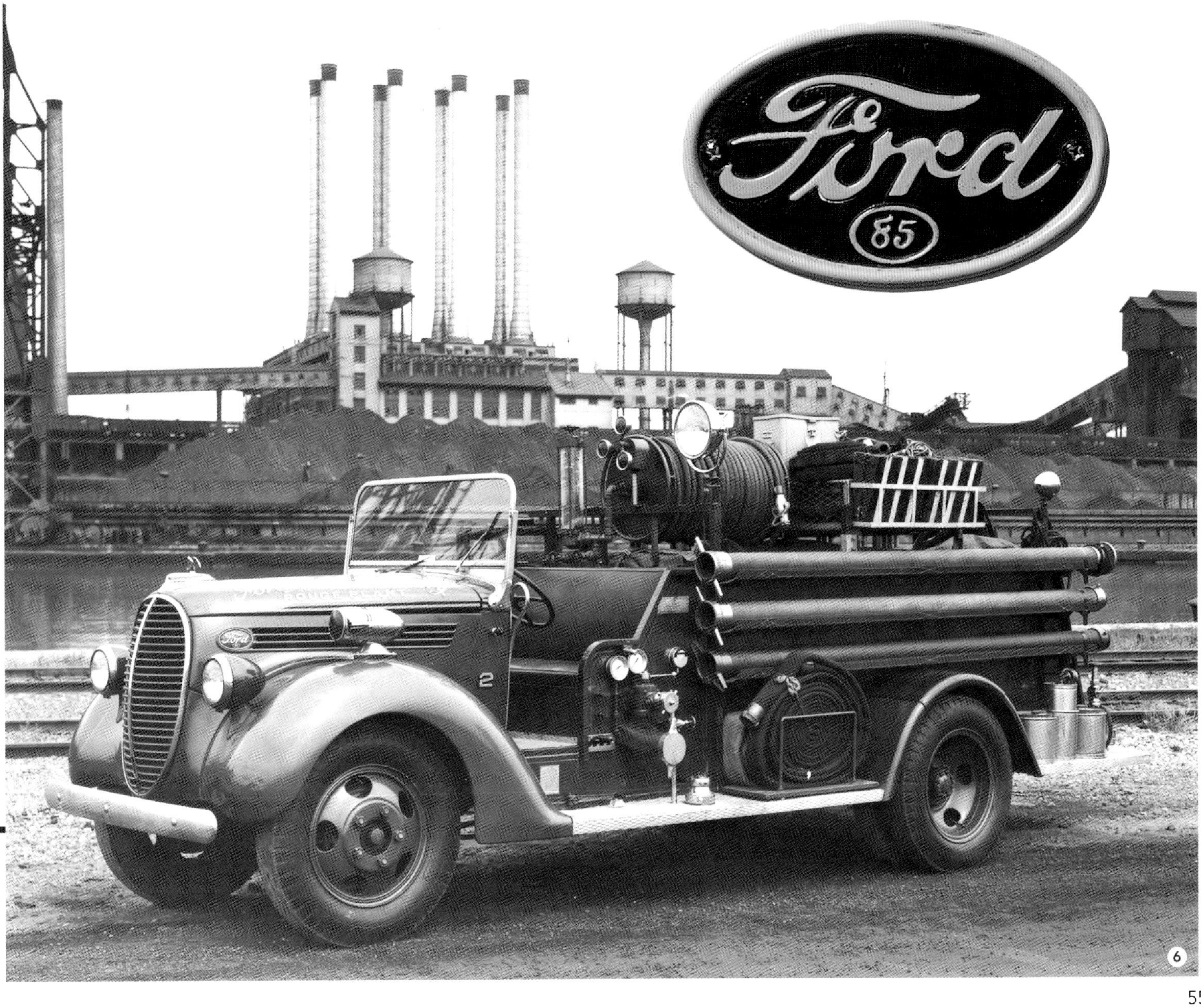

6

1939

1939: Years after most competitors had adopted them, Ford finally shifts to hydraulic brakes; Mercury brand debuts with a 239-cubic-inch flathead V-8 also newly available in trucks; cars again have different styling for base and Deluxe series; Three-Quarter-Tonner introduced; Ford reenters the tractor business; World War II begins in Europe

1. A 1939 COE Stake Bed truck serves as a rolling billboard for a beverage company, spreading the word that Pepsi hits the spot, Nehi comes in your favorite flavors, and Set-Up's "Lithiated Lemon" makes for a good mixer. The truck was probably also handy for deliveries. 2. A former Ford Rouge Plant fire truck—similar to that shown on the previous page—was later used in Flint, Michigan, for awhile before being restored to its original glory. 3-5. Though it looked little different than its 1938 counterpart, this '39 pickup boasts the unseen advantage of hydraulic brakes. Most competitors had adopted them years before, but Henry Ford had steadfastly stuck with the old mechanically actuated brakes until public and dealer pressure forced his hand. While car dashboards of the period began to show some semblance of "style," truck dashboards remained as flat and featureless as...well...a board.

Chapter Four: 1940-1949

A Roller-Coaster Ride

The 1940s can best be described as a roller-coaster ride for the Ford Motor Company. It would celebrate a number of high points during the decade, but would also have to endure its share of lows.

Things started out well for Ford, particularly when it came to its commercial vehicles. Practically all of them featured fresh styling cues, with lighter-duty models mimicking the look of their automotive cousins. Heavier-duty trucks—except for the Cab-Over-Engine models—were also restyled, though not in the same vein. All Ford regular-cab models used reworked cabs that incorporated a one-piece cowl top, roof, and windshield-pillar stamping. They also got a new instrument panel, along with sealed-beam headlights.

FORD
FORD

1940-1949

Chapter Four

The big news for 1941 was the availability of a new six-cylinder engine option to augment Ford's flathead V-8. The six had more torque than the V-8 and provided somewhat better fuel economy. And for those really interested in economy, also offered on some light- and medium-duty trucks during this period was a four-cylinder engine based on that of the company's farm tractor.

In war-related work, Ford began producing a version of the 4×4 "Jeep" type universal vehicle for the military, and also started constructing new war-related plants—just in case the United States got drawn into World War II.

Ford trucks were treated to a restyle for 1942 that was shared by all models, and they no longer looked like the car line. However, it turned out to be a short selling season.

The United States was drawn into World War II on December 7, 1941, shortly after Ford's 1942 models were introduced. The order was given to stop production of civilian vehicles on February 10, 1942, so assembly plants could be converted to producing war materiel. From the time the plants closed through to the end of the war, Ford concentrated its efforts into building B-24 Liberator bombers; aircraft engines; tanks; Jeep-type military vehicles; wooden gliders; and military versions of the 1942-era pickup trucks, cars, and heavy-duty trucks.

In May 1943, the Ford Motor Company suffered a heavy loss with the death of Edsel Ford, Henry's only son, who at the time was president of the company. Upon Edsel's death, Henry Ford once again stepped in to take the helm, but at 80 years of age, wasn't capable of the task. Because Ford Motor Company was so vital to the war effort, the United States government stepped in, essentially assigning a successor. Tapped for the job was Edsel's oldest son, Henry Ford II.

At the time, "Henry the Deuce" was in the Navy. At just 26 years of age, the government pulled him out of military service and reassigned him to the vice presidency of Ford Motor Company.

With demand for war-related vehicles easing toward the end of 1944, the War Production Board authorized Ford to resume production of a limited run of heavy-duty trucks for the civilian market. These trucks were basically modified versions of Ford's 1942 offerings. In order to be able to buy one, purchasers had to prove their business was vital to the war effort.

The War Production Board allowed

the automobile companies to produce more vehicles for the civilian market starting in early 1945. Ford took this cue to boost production of its heavy-duty trucks, which were introduced in May of that year. Though they looked like Ford's 1942 models, they were treated to a number of modifications, including an improved V-8 engine.

In September 1945, Henry Ford finally stepped down from leading the company that bore his name. As expected, he was succeeded in the presidency by his grandson, Henry Ford II.

What Henry II inherited was a company in rather dire straits. Ford Motor Company had been on unsteady financial footing before the war, and didn't emerge from it in any better shape. It would prove a formidable challenge to turn the company around, but its new president succeeded.

Ford's Cab-Over-Engine models returned to the lineup in 1946, and were joined by some heavier-duty two-ton models. These "Ford Heavies" featured reinforced frames, two-speed rear axles, heavier-duty springs, and larger tires.

On April 7, 1947, the company—and indeed, the country—mourned the loss of one of the automotive industry's great pioneers, when Henry Ford died at his home. He was 83.

In January 1948, a new era began at the Ford Motor Company with the release of an all-new line of trucks that Ford dubbed the "F-Series." This new series, which Ford promoted as its "Bonus Built Line," covered a wide range of models with different cab and chassis combinations. The line started out with light-duty ½-ton-rated pickup trucks and ran all the way up to the Extra Heavy-Duty, three-ton-rated F-8. These trucks used a completely redesigned cab with all-new front-end sheetmetal. And in a departure from previous practice, the same cab served both conventional and Cab-Over-Engine models.

For 1949, Ford restyled its car line for the first time since the war, but because it didn't include a Sedan Delivery model, the truck line was not affected. What the truck line did get, however, were a couple of new stand-up Parcel Delivery vehicles.

Looking back over the decade, Ford faced financial troubles and fought back with successful new products. Though the Forties will always be remembered as "The War Years," Ford produced some vehicles that would long be remembered as well.

1940

1940: ½-ton trucks take on car styling for first time since 1932; seven-millionth V-8 engine and 28-millionth Ford vehicle produced

For 1940, ½-ton pickups adopted the look of that year's Standard-series cars—the first time since 1932 that trucks shared car styling. This included a vee'd grille, pointed hood, and headlights mounted into the fenders, giving these haulers a modern, classy look. Power continued to come from a choice of two flathead V-8 engines: a 136-cubic-inch 60-horsepower unit, or a 221-cid 85-hp version.

1-2. By contrast, Sedan Deliveries carried the styling of Deluxe-series 1940 cars, with slated "gills" flanking a horizontal-bar grille. The interior was also new, and likewise followed the lead of its automotive counterparts with dressy two-toning and chrome accents. Sedan Deliveries also got a larger cargo body this year.
3. Panel Deliveries mirrored truck styling for 1940.

1940

Originally used by the Bell Telephone Co., this pickup sports a special utility box. Though the exterior mimicked car styling, the interior still said "truck" with its flat, monotone dashboard.

1941

1941: Ford adds six-cylinder engine option for cars and trucks; sized at 226 cubic inches, the six makes 90 horsepower—five more than the 221-cid V-8. Smaller 60-hp V-8 dropped, replaced by four-cylinder tractor engine that garnered little interest; car styling revised, but for first—and only—time, Sedan Delivery doesn't follow suit, retaining 1940 look; United States enters World War II on December 7

1. A 1941 COE flatbed gets loaded down with part of a ship's cargo. These trucks got a car-inspired grille for ′41 to replace the previous upright oval.

2. Conventional heavy-duty trucks retained the previous year's styling, as shown on this 1941 Stake Bed. Note that all heavy-duty models retained freestanding headlights.

1941

1. Ford-powered tractor-trailer rigs appeared in the late 1920s, and by the early Forties, were capable of pulling two heavily loaded trailers. 2. A shortened Ford one-ton chassis is seen fitted with a custom delivery body. Trucks used for local deliveries, such as this milk wagon, were sometimes ordered with 1941's newly available four-cylinder tractor engine for better fuel economy. 3. Due to wartime shortages of materials to make chrome plating, late-1941 vehicles came with painted trim, as seen on this mail truck. 4. There's little doubt as to the cargo carried by this ´41 Ford operated by the Dunham Ice Company of Baton Rouge, Louisiana.

1. Joy Farm of Milwaukee, Wisconsin, used a stable of Fords in its operation. Note the front-end treatment on the Station Wagon at left, which carried styling that was new to that year's car line. By this time, the Station Wagon was considered a car rather than a light commercial vehicle. 2. To many, the 1940 and little-changed ´41 pickups were among the best-looking Ford trucks ever built. This restored ´41 has been in the owner's family since new.

2

1942

1942: Civilian vehicle production ends on February 10; gas rationing begins

1-2. Ford trucks boasted new styling for 1942, but relatively few were built; production ceased on February 10, 1942, so the company could concentrate on building war materiel. 3-4. A Sedan Delivery shows off the redesign given Ford cars for 1942. Like their truck counterparts, car production was low—and for the same reason.

1942-44

1943-1944. Henry Ford II reassigned by the military to Detroit to watch over company; Ford concentrates on building war-related arms, vehicles, and equipment; Edsel Ford, Henry's only son, dies on May 26, 1943

1. Ford built several prototype ¾-ton military vehicles, including this forward-control four-wheel-drive cargo truck. 2. Like other Big-Three American manufacturers, Ford produced tanks during the war. Power came from an advanced 1100-cubic-inch, double-overhead-cam, four-valve-per cylinder, aluminum-block V-8, which was in stark contrast to the firm's antiquated cast-iron flathead V-8 used in passenger cars and trucks. 3. Ford was one of the manufacturers contracted to build prototypes of what the military referred to as the ¼-ton General Purpose vehicle. A prototype is shown during testing. Abbreviated "GP," the vehicle would later become known as the "Jeep."

1942-44

1. Ford turned out more than 270,000 of the Army's General Purpose vehicles during the war. These differed somewhat from Ford's prototypes, as the military adopted a design that was then built in nearly identical form by several companies. 2. Military brass are shown being chauffeured in a "Jeep." Note it is fitted with street tires as opposed to the heavily lugged off-road versions fitted to the production-line vehicles above.

1. A Ford-built 1942 GPW (General Purpose—Willys) restored to its wartime splendor. Thousands managed to return home after the conflict, and some unrestored examples are still used as everyday workhorses.
2-4. Ford produced a variety of military vehicles during World War II, and not all were land-based. Ads from the period extolled Ford's efforts, and included images of its trucks, tanks, and the twin-tail B-24 Liberator bomber.

1945-47

1945: World War II ends; limited civilian production resumes; Ford Motor Company builds the first vehicle and gives it to Harry Truman; Fords adopt Mercury's larger 239-cubic-inch V-8 in place of 221-cid unit; Henry Ford officially retires from Ford Motor Company; Henry Ford II takes over as company president

1947: Henry Ford dies on April 7 at age 83

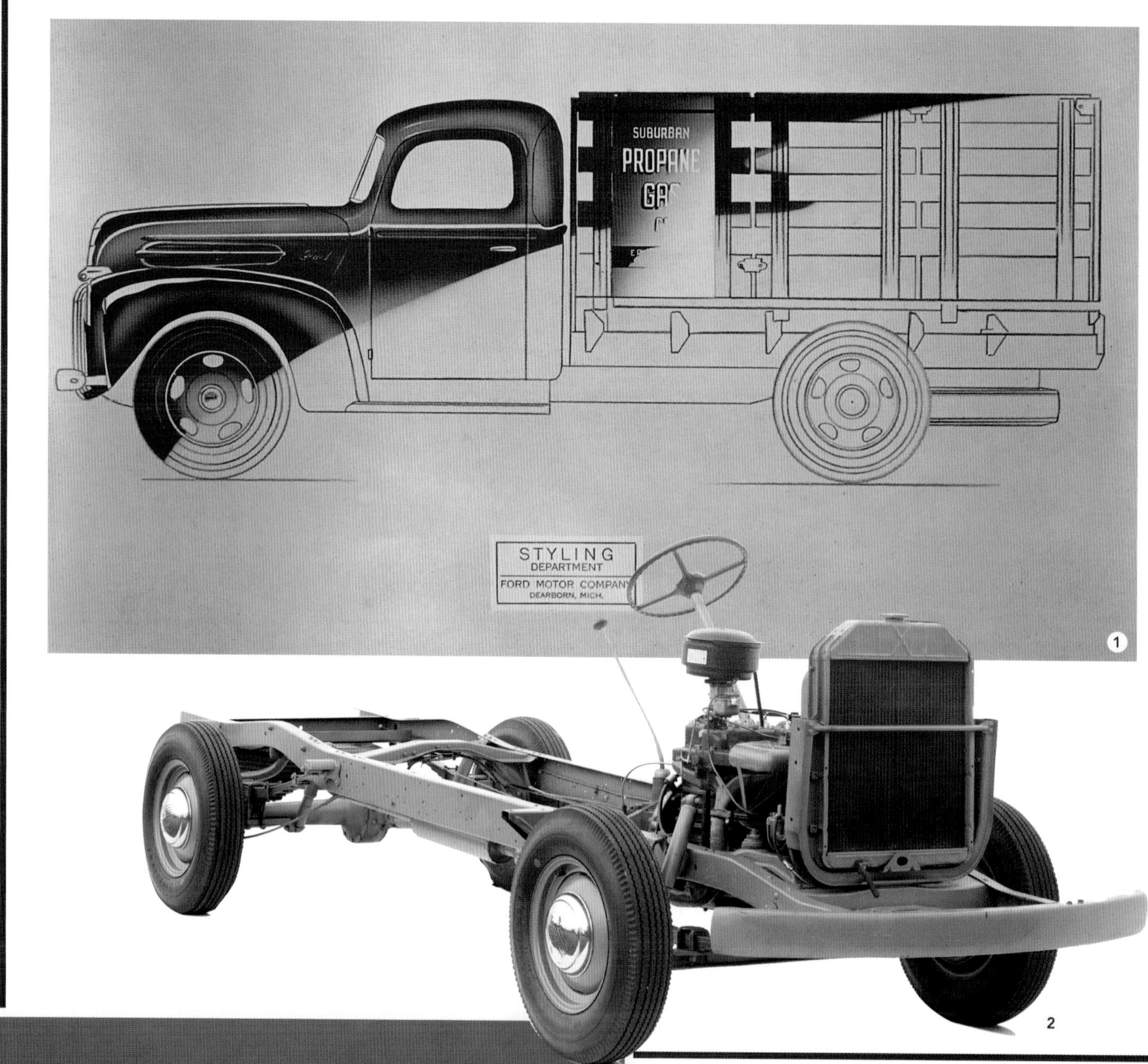

Production Resumes....................

Civilian vehicles—mostly trucks—trickled out of factories in early 1945, several months before the end of World War II. In fact, the "official" start of civilian production, on July 3, 1945, still preceded the war's end by a month. Not surprisingly, postwar styling was changed only in detail from that of the 1942 models, which had been redesigned for what turned out to be a shortened model year. More surprising was the retirement of the venerable 221-cubic-inch flathead V-8 that had powered Fords since 1932. In its place was the similar but larger 239-cid Mercury unit. Missing from the lineup were the Three-Quarter Tonners and the less-than-popular four-cylinder tractor engine that had been offered in prewar trucks.

1. An illustration from the styling department at Ford Motor Co. shows a postwar truck that was virtually identical to its prewar predecessor. 2. Little changed mechanically, either, aside from the substitution of Mercury's 100-horsepower 239-cubic-inch flathead V-8 for the 90-hp 221-cid version used during the shortened 1942 model year. 3. New Era potato chips were delivered—and promoted—by this 1946 one-ton truck, which was now referred to by the factory as a "Tonner."

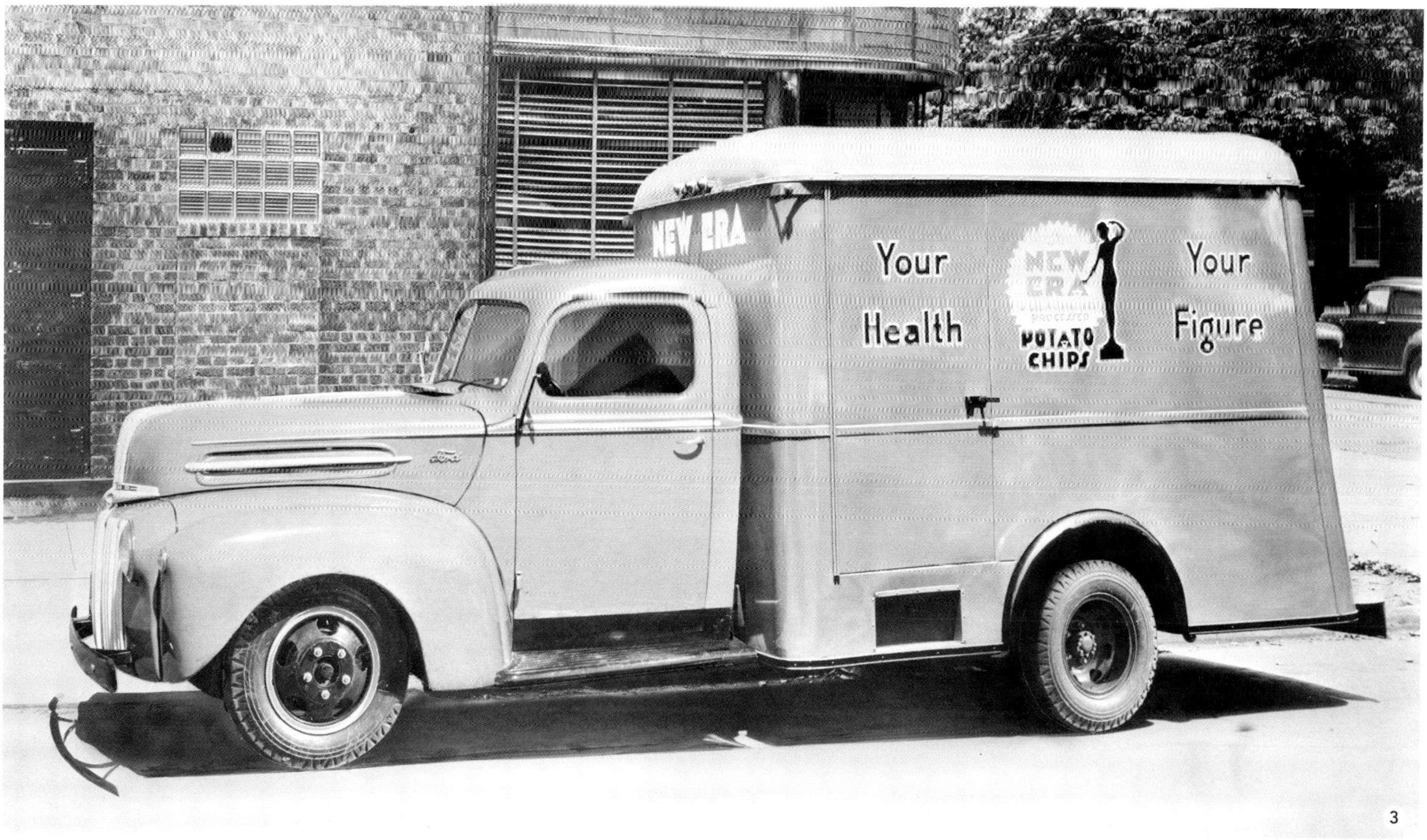

3

4

5

6

4-5. A Panel Delivery shows off its postwar face, which was little different from its prewar look. Note the "spare tire," that is just a wheel; even after the war, rubber supplies were short, and many vehicles didn't come with a mounted tire. 6. Similarly tire-less is this '46 ½-ton pickup, now called a "Half-Ton" by Ford.

1948

1948: Completely restyled trucks appear, beating redesigned postwar cars to market by a year; new model designations introduce the F-Series nomenclature that would carry on for decades, branding the ½-ton an F-1, the ¾-ton an F-2, the one-ton an F-3; 2 ½- and three-ton Extra Heavy Duty models, F-7 and F-8, respectively, added with larger 337-cubic-inch, 145-horsepower flathead V-8

Along with the fresh styling given 1948 Ford trucks came new model designations; this ½-ton was labeled the F-1. Squared-off front fenders wrapped smoothly into the front fascia, which contained a prominent horizontal-bar grille. Rear fenders were styled to match the profile of the fronts. Also new was a one-piece windshield.

1948

Excitingly MODERN! Strikingly DIFFERENT!

☆ **2 NEW BIG JOBS!**
Biggest Ford Trucks ever built! 145 H.P. engine! Up to 21,500 lbs. G.V.W.! Up to 10.00-20 tires!

☆ **NEW MILLION DOLLAR TRUCK CAB!**
With living room comfort! Biggest contribution to driver comfort in 20 years! New 3-way air control. New coach-type seats. New picture-window visibility! New Level Action cab suspension!

☆ **3 NEW TRUCK ENGINES!**
A new Six, two new V-8's! Most modern engine line in the truck field! Up to 145 H.P.! High turbulence combustion chambers! New Loadomatic ignition! 4-ring pistons!

☆ **OVER 139 NEW MODELS!**
Widest job coverage in Ford Truck history! Cab-Over-Engine and conventional chassis! Panel, Pickup, Express, Stake and Platform bodies! G.V.W. ratings 4,700 lbs. up to 21,500 lbs.

Listen to the Ford Theater over NBC stations Sunday afternoons, 5:00 to 6:00 p. m., E. S. T.

Hottest truck line in history . . . from the Leader in Trucks Built and Trucks in Use!

Our trucks are red-hot! That's because they're brand new! Ford *Bonus Built* Trucks for '48 are brand new in every important way but one!

Big exception is truck-building know-how! That isn't new with us! We've been building trucks for over 30 years! We've built more trucks and picked up more truck know-how than anyone else!

From a combination of the NEW in truck engineering and the KNOW-HOW of truck experience, you get new thrift! . . . new performance! . . . new reliability!

In Ford Trucks you get *Bonus Built* construction, the extra strength that pays off two ways. First, Ford *Bonus Built* Trucks are not limited to just one job, but are good all-around workers in a wide range of jobs. Second, Ford Trucks last longer. Life insurance experts *certify* proof that Ford Trucks last up to 19.6% longer!

Drop in on your Ford Dealer to size-up the new engines . . . new cabs . . . new BIG JOBS . . . over 139 new models in the biggest Ford Truck line in history!

*BONUS: "Something given in addition to what is usual or strictly due."—Webster's Dictionary

BUILT STRONGER TO LAST LONGER

To clearly identify its expanding line of trucks, Ford put the series identification on the cowl, just ahead of the door; this F-1's ID can be seen just above the trailing edge of the front fender. Less well-publicized was the engine beneath the hood, which in lighter-duty models could be either the 226-cubic-inch six-cylinder with 95 horsepower, or a 239-cid flathead V-8 with 100 hp. Ford promoted its redesigned "Bonus Built" line with splashy ads that contained a truckload of exclamation points.

1. Ads promoting Ford's heavy-duty trucks included mention of the new 337-cubic-inch flathead V-8 found in the equally new F-7 (2½-ton) and F-8 (three-ton) Extra Heavy Duty models. This engine put out an impressive (for the time) 145 horsepower—fully 45 percent more than the carryover 239-cubic-inch V-8 offered in Ford's smaller trucks. 2. From front bumper to rear, the Panel Truck was completely new for '48, as the body aft of the windshield was also redesigned. Cargo volume increased, as did the size of the rear access doors.

1

2

1948

1. A 1 ½-ton-rated F-5 chassis was fitted with a special body for this Coca-Cola distributor. 2. An F-8, Ford's largest truck, was advertised as having only a three-ton capacity, but its GVW rating allowed it to tip the scales at up to 21,500 lbs. 3. A cross-section illustration of Ford's V-8 shows the side-mounted valves and oddly shaped combustion chamber inherent in flathead designs. 4. Compared with today's trucks, those of the 1940s had a decidedly different seat/steering-wheel relationship, with the wheel being mounted closer to the driver in a more horizontal position. Note that dashboards on the new trucks were still rather plain.

3

4

1-4. Stake Bed trucks were available in both conventional (top and above) and COE (right and middle right) designs. The conventionals are 1½-ton F-5s, the COEs two-ton F-6s. Both could be powered by a 95-horsepower 226-cubic-inch six or a 100-hp 239-cid V-8.

1949

1949: Cars receive first postwar restyle, but with the demise of the Sedan Delivery after the war, truck lineup is not affected

1. The sensuous lines of this beauty appeared on a 1949 Ford pinup poster. Also visible in the foreground is a young lass.
2. All trucks shared the same corporate "face" of the 1948 redesign, regardless of chassis setup or weight class. So even vehicles such as this new-for-'49 Parcel Delivery chassis, which started with just a front end and windshield (the body being added by an aftermarket supplier), could easily be identified as a Ford.

1949

1-2, 5. A restored 1949 F-1 Panel Truck shows this captivating workhorse in all its original glory. The passenger seat was an option. 3-4. A generation of postwar baby boomers remember the ringing bell that accompanied the summertime arrival of the Good Humor truck. Most of these mobile ice cream trucks were Ford F-1 Chassis with Windshield models fitted with a special ice-box. 6-9. Perhaps one of the classic pickups of all time, the F-1 was a study of simplicity with style. Unlike some earlier Ford trucks, there was no external badging to indicate this restored example carries a V-8 rather than the standard six.

5

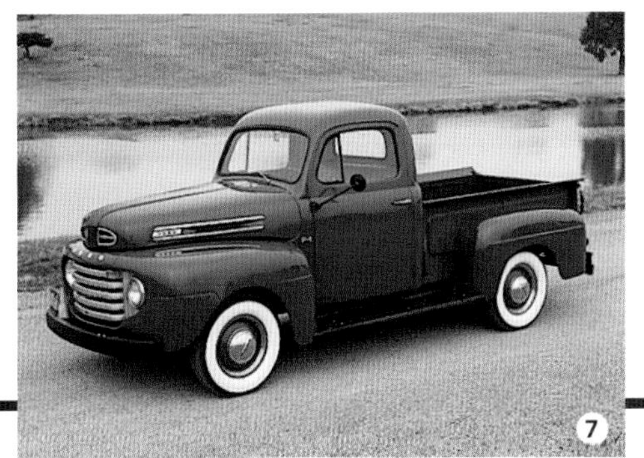

Chapter Five: 1950-1959

Getting Stylish, Adding Models, and Introducing a Car/Truck Hybrid

As flashy as Ford trucks would get in the late Fifties, those that ushered in the decade could only be described as subdued—and little-changed from the year before. Aside from a larger "Big Six" engine for F-6 buyers who didn't want to opt for the V-8, there wasn't much new and exciting for dealers to trumpet.

Not so for 1951, which saw a number of revisions. Restyled for the first time since their 1948 debut, Ford's F-Series conventionals and C-Series Cab-Over-Engine trucks received modified front fenders, grille cavity, and grille. Also changed were the hoods and cabs, along with the dashboard and rear window, which was now substantially larger for better visibility.

Also for '51—and for the first time since the late 1930s—Ford offered truck buyers two levels of cab trim: the standard Five Star Cab, and the deluxe Five Star Extra Cab. The latter came with such niceties as foam seat padding, extra sound deadening material, bright metal trim around the windshield and vent windows, an argent-finished grille bar, locks and armrests on both doors, two-toned seat upholstery, a dome light, and twin horns.

Ford introduced new overhead-valve engines for 1952, but not all made it to the truck line—at least, not yet. The first new ohv engine, a six-cylinder displacing 215 cubic inches, was available in Ford trucks from the F-1 through the F-5, as well as Ford cars. The second was a large

1950-1959

Chapter Five

V-8 based on a new Lincoln engine that was offered in 279- or 317-cubic-inch variations, but it was only available in the big F-7 and F-8 models; smaller trucks still used the old flathead V-8.

Ford Motor Company celebrated its Golden Anniversary in 1953 by introducing a totally redesigned line of F-Series trucks. The company also took this opportunity to change its model designations, adding "00" to the end of the existing monikers. Thus the F-1 became the F-100, and so on—the nomenclature still used today. Added at the top of the line was a new heavy-duty model called the F-900.

Instead of calling these trucks the "Bonus Built" models, as they had been from 1948 to1952, Ford now referred to them as the "Economy Truck Line." Joining the new name was a new hood emblem: a gear cog bisected by a lightning bolt below the Ford script. And for the first time in Ford-truck history, an automatic transmission was offered as an option, though initially only on F-100s.

Nineteen fifty-four brought the end of Ford's famous flathead V-8, replaced in trucks that year by the overhead-valve V-8 already two years old in Ford's car line. Referred to as the "Y-Block" engine, it displaced the same 239 cubic inches as the flathead, but produced nearly 15 percent more horsepower.

Another first for Ford trucks in '54 was the availability of tandem rear-axle setups for heavy-duty work. Ford referred to these trucks as the T-700 and T-800 models. Ford also added a couple of heavy-duty Cab-Over-Engine models in the form of the C-700 and C-900. Also that year, availability of the automatic-transmission option was expanded to include F-250 and F-350 trucks.

Most of the news coming out of Ford Motor Company in 1955 centered on the redesigned car line and the introduction of a new sporty personal car named Thunderbird. As for trucks, changes were kept to a minimum, with little beside revised grille and exterior trim pieces.

That changed for 1956, at least to a degree. Ford gave trucks a wraparound windshield that provided a fresh look—but not as fresh as they'd be for '57.

Rival General Motors had brought out stylish new trucks for 1955, and for two years, Ford had to face the competition with a warmed-over line that dated back to 1953. That made 1957 a very big year for Ford dealers, as they finally had a stylish truck of their own. Two, actually.

Ford's F-Series now sported a completely new look that was more square and modern, while at the same time featuring a wider cab; hidden running boards; flush-mounted front fenders; and a wider, full-width hood. The year also brought a choice of two pickup beds: the traditional Flareside, with a narrow bed and attached rear fenders; and the new Styleside, with straight-through fenders. A straight-sided bed was nothing new to the industry, but unlike other manufacturers, Ford offered its Styleside pickup box at no extra charge.

Perhaps even bigger news was the new car/truck hybrid called the Ranchero. Based on a two-door station-wagon platform, it combined Ford's new-for-'57 car styling with the utility of a pickup by replacing the wagon's covered cargo area with an open bed.

In addition to the dramatic changes that greeted pickup buyers this year, Ford also performed a major revamp to its Cab-Over-Engine models. These C-Series trucks were converted to a forward-control design, placing the steering wheel and pedals ahead of the axle, and the driver seat above it. They were branded "Tilt Cabs" because their cabs tilted forward for easier engine access.

Though the major 1958 news stories at Ford Motor Company were the introduction of the ill-fated Edsel and a more successful four-passenger replacement for the two-seat Thunderbird, trucks got some changes as well. Like their automotive counterparts, nearly all Ford trucks were restyled to accommodate quad headlights. But the big change—literally—was a new line of heavier-duty models called Super Duty, which came equipped with new V-8 engines of up to a whopping 534 cubic inches.

For the first time in Ford history, a light-duty truck buyer could buy a factory-built 4×4 in 1959. Previously, Ford trucks were converted to four-wheel drive by outside manufacturers such as Marmon-Herrington, Napco, or American-Coleman. Nineteen fifty-nine also brought a redesigned Ranchero, which again echoed the look of the equally redesigned car line. As it would turn out, this would be the last year the Ranchero would be based on a full-size station-wagon chassis.

Also in 1959, Ford celebrated a production milestone when its 50-millionth car—a Galaxie hardtop—left a company assembly plant. Ford cars outsold those of rival Chevrolet that year, putting a finishing touch on what had been an exciting decade.

1950

1950: Trucks and cars change little, though latter now wear new Ford Crest badges that wouldn't grace trucks for a few more years; North Korea invades South Korea, sparking the Korean War; Clara Ford, Henry's widow, dies

Since its redesign two years earlier, the F-1 had received only detail changes, none of which are readily visible on this 1950 model. Power comes from Ford's 226-cubic-inch flathead six rated at 95 horsepower. Note that this example has a floor-mounted shifter, which was being phased out in favor of column shift.

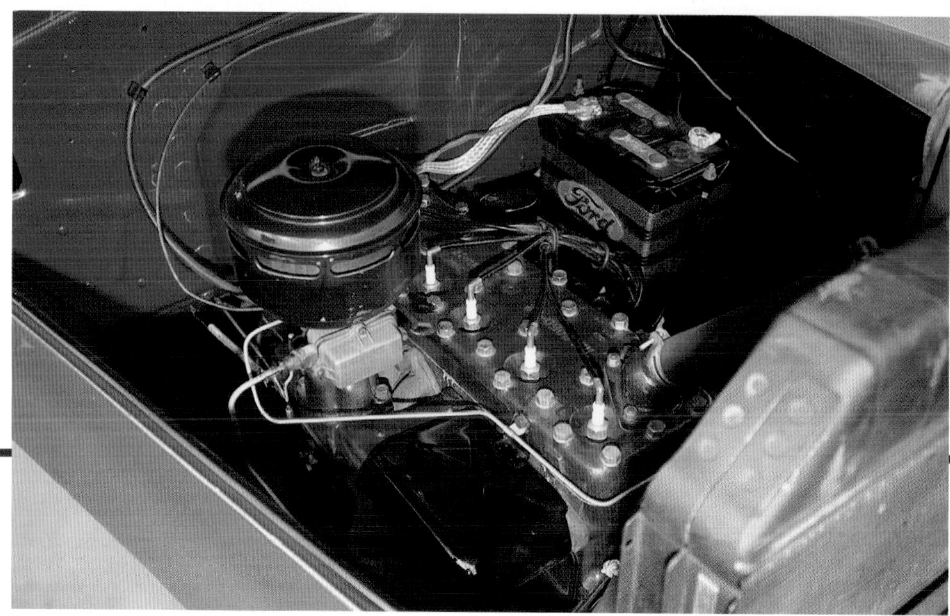

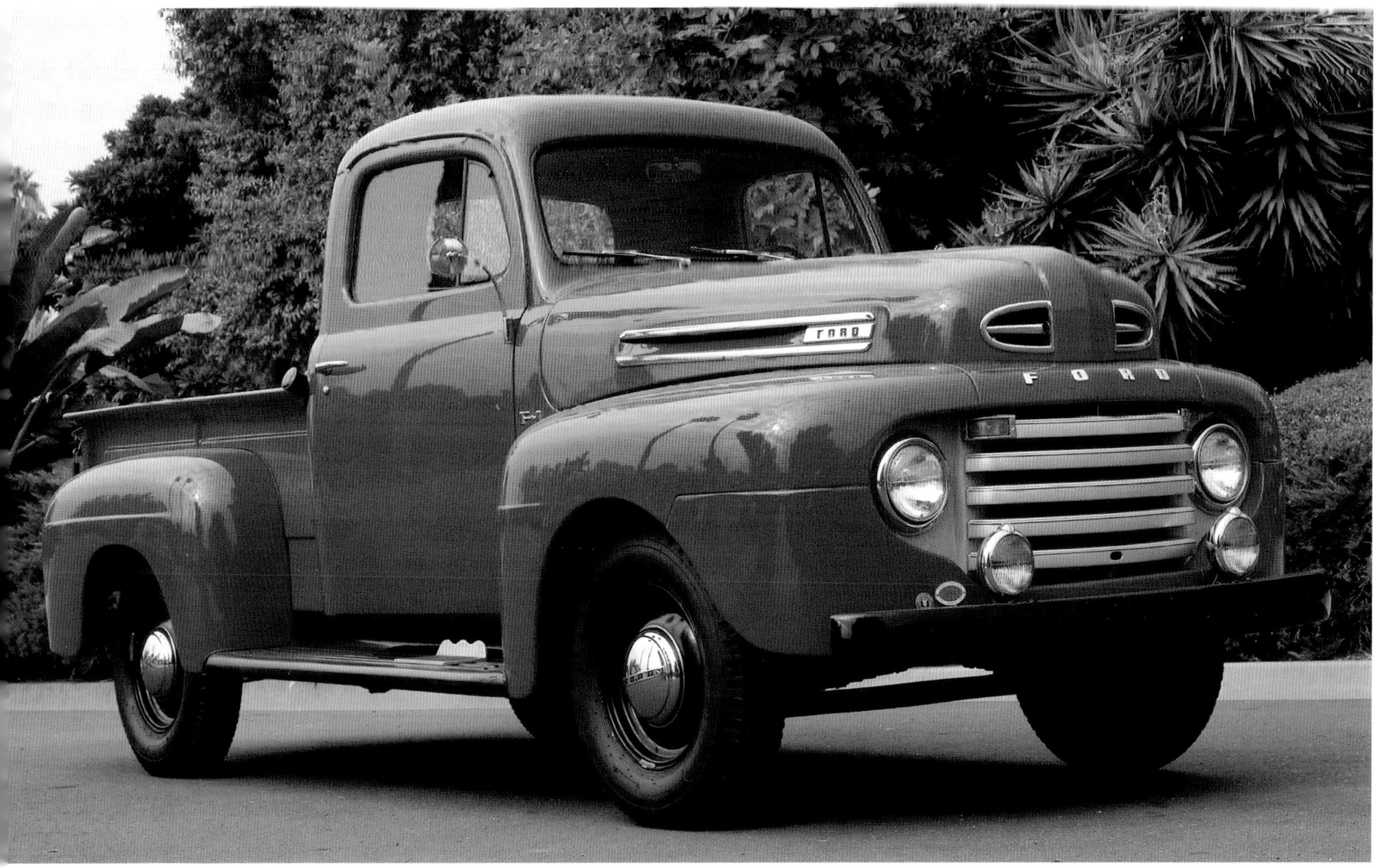
FORD
FORD

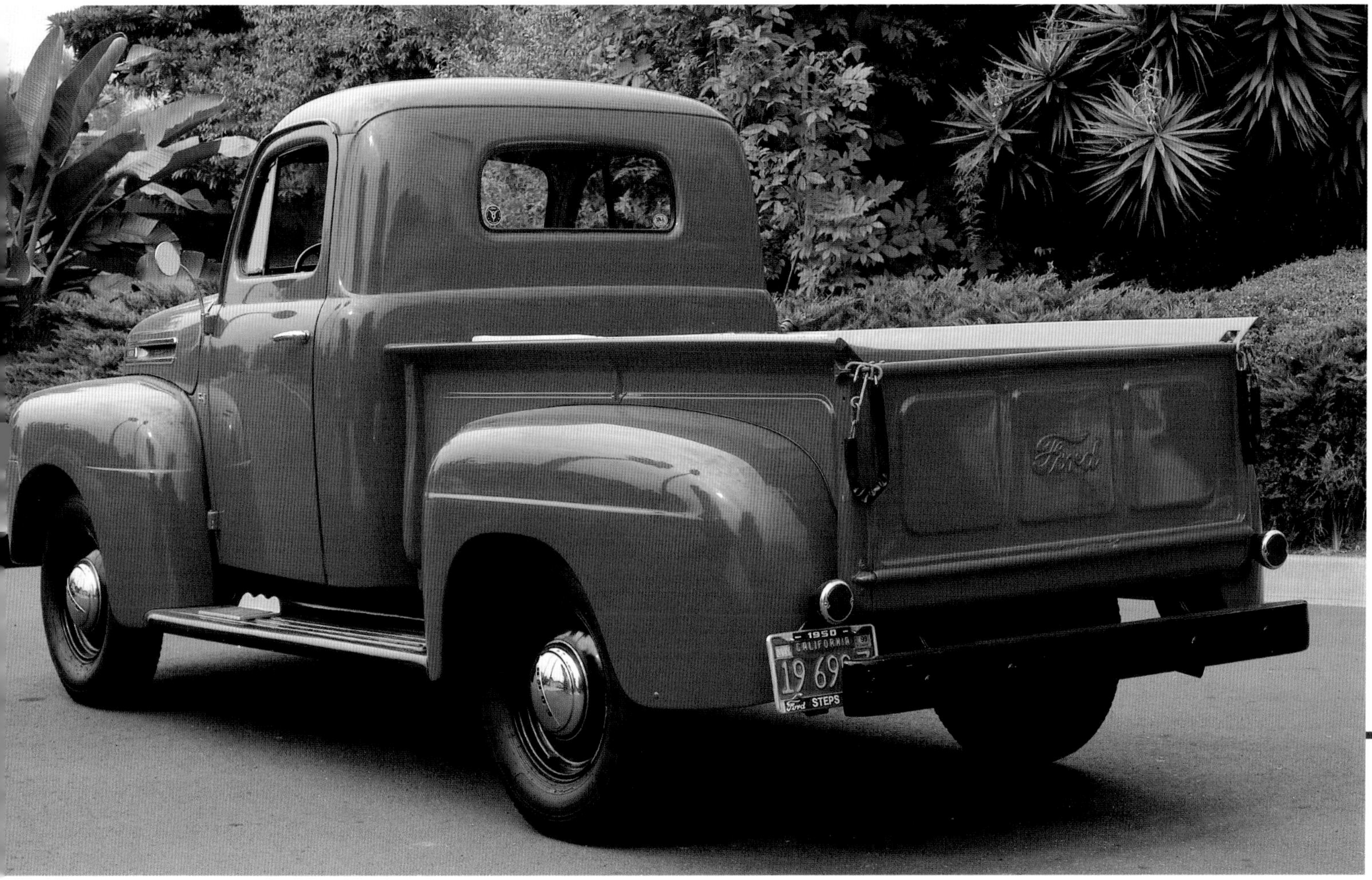
1950
CALIFORNIA
STEPS

1950

1

2

1. Wearing an unusually sleek body by Howe, this restored 1950 Ford F-7 pumper was originally used by Martin Township in Michigan. 2. Since their '48 redesign, Panel Trucks had only been offered in ½-ton F-1 versions. 3. An army of Good Humor drivers prepares to fight summer's heat with a fleet of Ford F-1 pickups converted for their intended use.

3

1. A Ford F-5 totes a reproduction of the Liberty Bell in a promotion intended to encourage the purchase of U.S. Savings Bonds with the tagline, "Save for YOUR Independence." 2. Newly optional on F-6s for 1950 was a 254-cubic-inch six-cylinder engine rated at 110 horsepower, which would surely be helpful in hauling the heavy loads this Stake Bed truck could carry.

1951

1951: F-Series receives its first facelift

1-2. Resplendent in its cherry-red paint, whitewall tires, and chrome trim, this restored 1951 F-1 looks ready for a night on the town; most pickups of the era weren't dressed nearly as well. It shows off that year's new look, with revised front fascia, grille, and hood trim. Pickup beds now had a wood floor rather than steel, and note the larger rear window that accompanied the 1951 redesign. As advertised on its nose, it carries Ford's 239-cubic-inch flathead V-8, still rated at 100 horsepower. 3. Another change for '51 was that the F-Series designation no longer appeared on the cowl, as evidenced by this F-1 Panel Truck. Instead, it was stamped into the leading edge of the hood's side-trim "spear." 4. Popular with farmers, an F-5 could be fitted with a nine- or 12-foot Stake Body.

4

1951

1

2

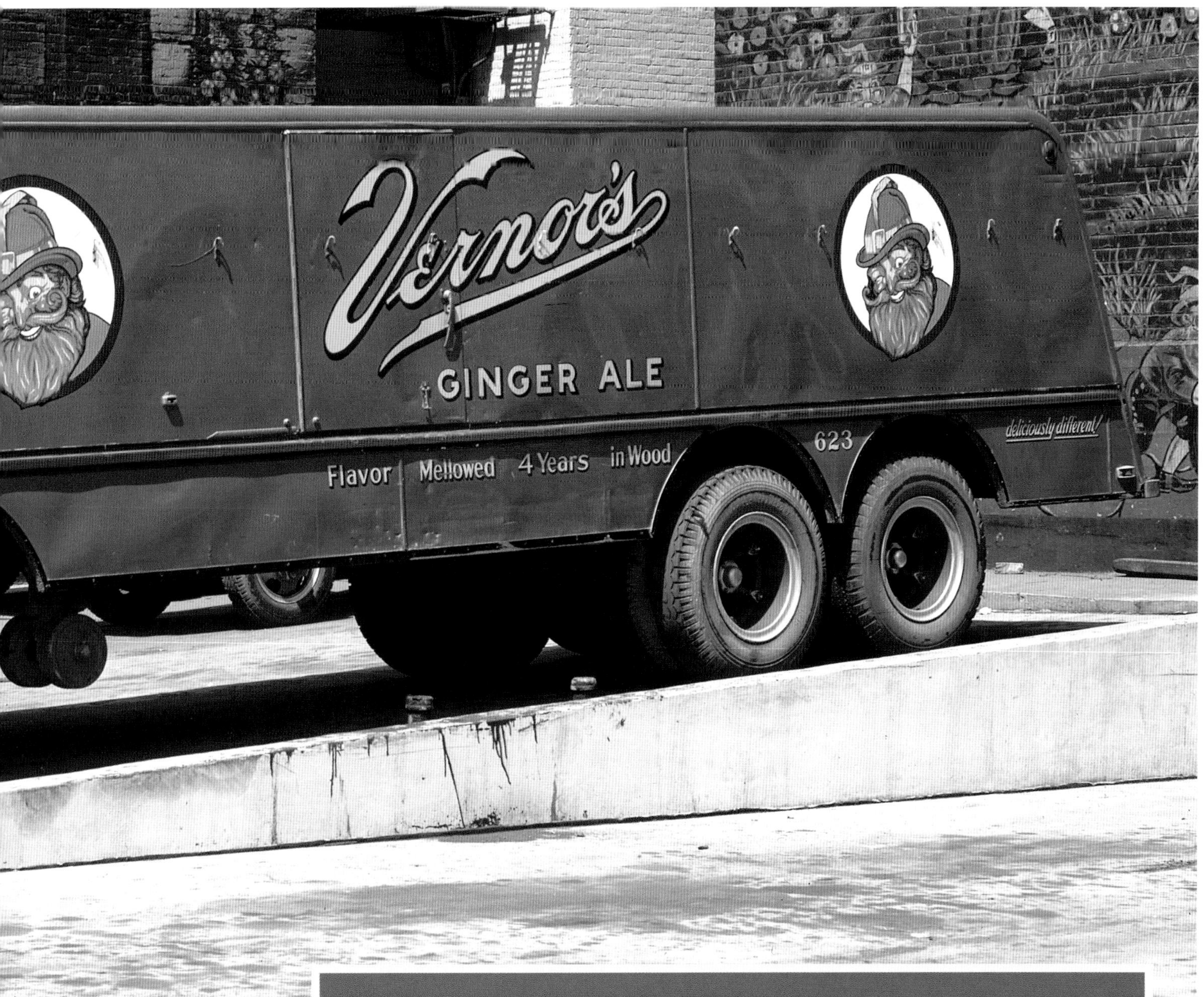

1. A 1951 F-8 tractor hauls a trailer load of Vernor's ginger ale. It is fitted with the cast wheels and demountable rims newly available that year. 2. Another F-8 tractor sports special wheels that combine a demountable-rim feature with a standard eight-lug bolt pattern. It also has an aftermarket dual-rear-axle conversion that allowed for a higher-than-stock GVW.

Heavy Haulers...

Ford's Extra Heavy Duty F-7 and F-8 models were called "Big Jobs," and indeed, that's what they could do. These were the only two F-Series models fitted with Ford's big 336-cubic-inch flathead V-8, which was available with an exclusive five-speed transmission.

At first, all Big Jobs were fitted with eight-lug steel wheels, but in 1951, Ford began offering cast wheels with demountable rims. This allowed tractor-trailer units with demountable rims to use the same spare tire on any wheel. Also new that year was an available two-speed rear axle.

Though the F-8 carried a three-ton rating, it had a Gross Vehicle Weight (GVW) of 21,500 lbs. And some aftermarket companies offered a tandem rear suspension (a second rear axle) that allowed for even higher payloads. For tractors hauling trailers, the F-8 offered a Gross Combined Weight (GCW) of up to 39,000 lbs.

1952

1952: Ford introduces new overhead-valve six- and eight-cylinder engines; Sedan Delivery returns, carrying new-for-'52 car styling

1

1-5. Truck styling was altered little for 1952, with the most noticeable change affecting the nose and side trim on the hood. Beneath the hood was a different story, however, as a new six-cylinder engine boasting overhead valves was introduced. Sized at 215 cubic inches, it produced 101 horsepower, six more than the 226-cid flathead six it replaced. The flathead V-8 continued in Ford pickups as before, though cars and heavy-duty trucks offered overhead-valve V-8s. 6. Ford's car line received its second postwar redesign for 1952, and this time a Sedan Delivery was included in the mix. 7. Marmon-Harrington had long been offering four-wheel-drive conversions for Ford trucks. When a '52 Panel Delivery was so equipped, it was called a "Ranger."

1

1952

2

3

4

1-2. The rearmost banner on the cargo-body "spine" of this 1952 F-5 reminds fans to drink Dr. Pepper at 10, 2, and 4 o'clock. 3. The F-6 chassis-cab weighed 4590 lbs and had a GVW rating of up to 16,000 lbs. Its V-8 was still the venerable 239-cubic-inch flathead, rated at 110 horsepower. 4. Available on F-7 "Big Job" trucks was a new overhead-valve V-8 of 279 cid and 145 hp. F-8s got an even larger version, at 317 cid and 155 hp.

1953

1953: Ford celebrates its Golden Anniversary; trucks redesigned, getting new series designations; automatic transmission offered in light-duty pickups; Korean War ends

In their first redesign since 1948, Ford's trucks received a longer hood that flowed into the front fenders, along with horizontal grille bars. Cabs were also new, boasting more glass area.

1953

1-4. A set-back front axle made the '53s look nose-heavy but allowed for a tighter turning radius. Series designations added "00" to the end, meaning this light-duty pickup went from being an F-1 to being an F-100. Nineteen fifty-three was the first year an automatic transmission was available in trucks (In the F-100 line), but would prove to be the final year for the flathead V-8. 5. The former F-4 continued its one-ton rating as the F-350. This nomenclature is still used today. 6. New front turn signals and grille crossbar mark this Sedan Delivery as a '53. Late in the model year, power steering was offered for the first time.

1

1953

2

3

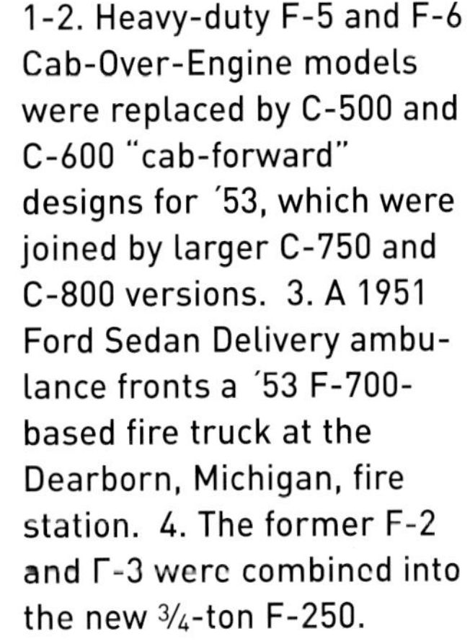

1-2. Heavy-duty F-5 and F-6 Cab-Over-Engine models were replaced by C-500 and C-600 "cab-forward" designs for ′53, which were joined by larger C-750 and C-800 versions. 3. A 1951 Ford Sedan Delivery ambulance fronts a ′53 F-700-based fire truck at the Dearborn, Michigan, fire station. 4. The former F-2 and F-3 were combined into the new 3/4-ton F-250.

4

1953

1

1-2. Ford's Big Job models became the F-700, F-750, and F-800. The 700 and 750 had the same 19,500-lb GVW rating, but the former was powered by a six-cylinder engine, the latter by a V-8. Added for ´53 was a new F-900, which offered a GVW of 27,000 lbs.

2

1954

1954: After more than 20 years, the flathead V-8 is finally retired, replaced by a more powerful overhead-valve V-8; automatic transmission offered in more models; tandem-axle trucks introduced; minor changes to grille

1. Another grille change marked Ford's 1954 trucks, this time adding a pair of prominent vertical guards. The V-8 badge on the grille indicates this pickup has Ford's new overhead-valve V-8. At 239 cubic inches, displacement was the same as the flathead's, but horsepower rose from 110 to 130. 2. Ford introduced a pair of tandem-rear-axle models in 1953, the T-700 and T-800. Previously, buyers wanting a tandem-axle chassis had to have it built using an aftermarket conversion kit.

1954

1

2

3

4

1-4. A cross in the center of its grille indicates this restored F-100 carries the revised six-cylinder engine Ford issued for 1954. A bore increase brought it up to 223 cubic inches and 115 horsepower from 215 cid/101 hp. The six chrome hash marks that flank the cross indicate this is a Deluxe model, which had fancier trim. Adopted with the ′53 redesign was a new hood badge featuring a lightning-bolt/gearwheel motif below the famous Ford script. 5-7. A step up from the light-duty F-100 was the ¾-ton F-250. As identified by the grille markings, this is a standard-trim version with the new-for-'54 overhead-valve V-8. Ford expanded availability of the optional automatic transmission for 1954, offering it for F-250s and F-350s in addition to the F-100s.

1955

1955: Power brakes and tubeless tires debut; grille again restyled; car line redesigned, bringing a new Sedan Delivery, now called the Courier

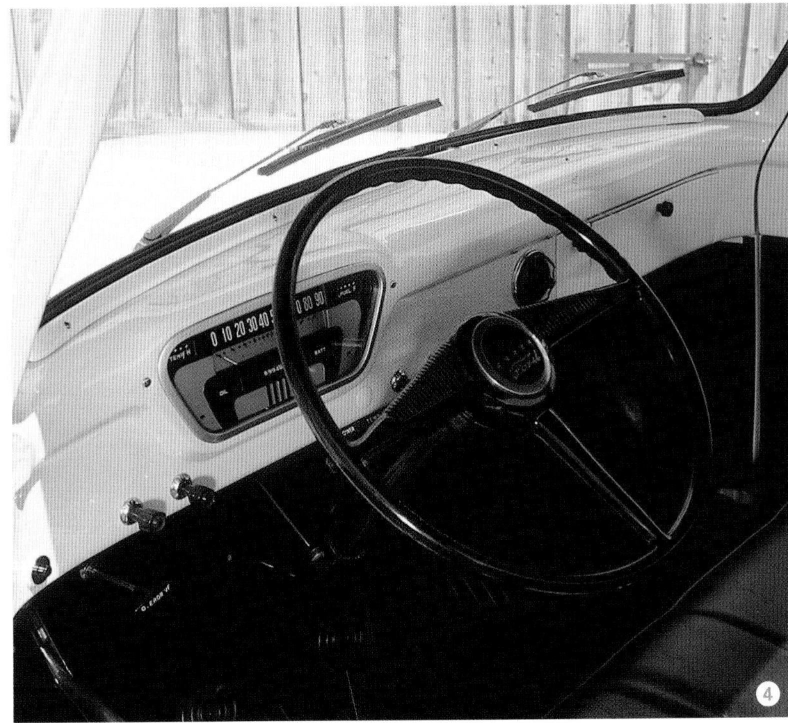

1. Yet another change to grille design differentiated the 1955 Ford trucks from the ´54s. The vertical guards were dropped in favor of a vee-shaped dip in the upper bar, which again carried an indicator of six-cylinder or V-8 engine. Less obvious were the switch to tubeless tires on F-100s and the newly optional power brakes. 2. A 1955 F-800 Big Job dump truck boasts the tandem-axle setup introduced in ´54, which was becoming very popular. 3-5. Not surprisingly, the F-100 with 6 ½-foot bed was Ford's most popular truck in 1955. Despite all the emphasis placed on exterior styling over the years, interiors had gained little in the way of "character" by that time.

1956

1956: Wraparound windshields introduced; tubeless-tire availability expanded to include F-250-and-up trucks; larger V-8s offered; Highway Act authorizes building of 41,000-mile Interstate Highway System, a boon to both drivers and construction companies

1. Ford offered larger V-8 engines for 1956, with a 302-cubic-inch version being available in heavy-duty trucks like this F-750 Stake Bed.
2. A lineup of 1956 Ford trucks extends from F-100 pickup and panel at right, through heavy-duty conventionals, to Big Job cab-forwards.

1956

In an effort to match the redesigned Chevrolet trucks that appeared for 1955, Ford attempted to modernize its F-Series by giving them wraparound windshields and restyled dashboards. Grilles got the customary annual update, now boasting a "Back to the Future" look very similar to that of the '53 models. A larger 272-cubic-inch V-8 offered 167 horsepower.

CALIFORNIA
A 56PKUP

1957

1957: All trucks redesigned; Styleside beds introduced; forward-control models replace cab-forward; car-based Ranchero debuts

A splashy two-page ad announces the arrival of the all-new 1957 lineup of Ford pickups, including Styleside models and the car-based Ranchero.

. . Only Ford offers 5 ½-ton Pickups for '57

This year, the big news—*the big choice*—in pickup trucks comes from Ford! For '57, Ford gives you a choice of five different pickups in the half-ton field alone. And in every model, the boldly modern styling merely hints at the *deep-down* modern design, with great new advances in power, comfort and ride. Make your selection at your Ford Dealer's today!

New Ford Ranchero! A real packhorse that hauls over half a ton! Lowest of all pickups, it looks, rides and handles like a car!

miest,
! New
ydrau-
dals!

For '57—and the years ahead

FORD TRUCKS COST LESS

...LESS TO OWN...LESS TO RUN...LAST LONGER, TOO!

Ford's radically redesigned F-Series offered slab-sided styling both front and rear for 1957 with the introduction of the Styleside bed. A traditional bed with separate fenders, called Flareside, was still available. Both beds were offered in 6 ½- and 8-foot lengths. Engine choices included a 223-cubic-inch six with 139 horsepower, and a 272-cid V-8 with 171 hp.

1957

1-3. The new Ranchero was a sensation, sharing the look of Ford's restyled 1957 cars. Top engine was the car line's 292-cubic-inch 212-horsepower V-8, which wasn't offered in other trucks. Ranchero was considered a ½-ton pickup like the F-100, but its styling and carlike amenities didn't come free; prices started at $2098, whereas an F-100—either Styleside or Flareside—started at $1789. 4. The Courier, which had been called a Sedan Delivery prior to 1955, was available with rear windows for 1957. It was essentially Ford's two-door, six-passenger Ranch Wagon station wagon without the rear seat.

1957

1. Heavy-duty trucks, as demonstrated by this T-750 tandem-axle prototype, also benefited from '57's new styling. 750s came with a 302-cubic-inch V-8 with 196 horsepower. 2. New for '57 were the C-Series Tilt Cab forward-control trucks, which would go on to live a long and prosperous life. Cabs could be tilted forward for easy engine access, and the set-back front axle allowed for a tight turning radius. Best of all, the design allowed for a shorter overall length with a given trailer size. Shown is the top-line C-900, which—like other 900s—used a 332-cubic-inch V-8 with 212 horsepower.

1958

1958: Quad headlights adopted; huge new truck engines introduced

1-2. Like most manufacturers, Ford switched to quad headlights for 1958, applying them to both cars and trucks. For the F-Series, that meant a restyled grille—which they had been getting every year anyway. By this time, interiors were beginning to show some style themselves, with contoured dashboards and carlike instrument panels. 3-4. The Ranchero returned for ´58 with a whole new face, necessitated in part by the move to quad headlights. With the change came a fancier, massive grille topped by a small hood scoop. Ford advertised the Ranchero as a truck for both work and play.

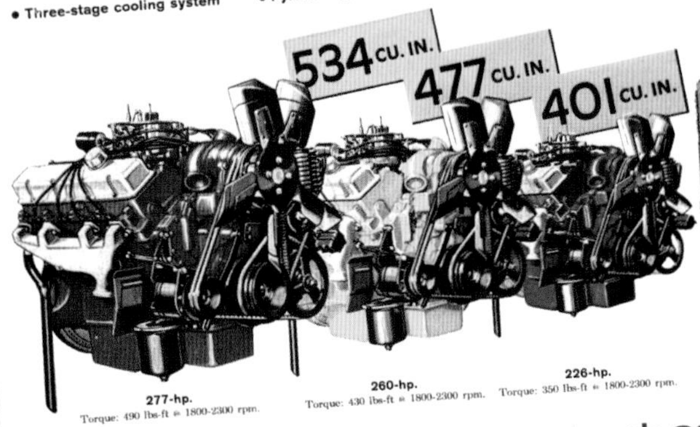

1958

Big power was the big news for Ford's 1958 Extra Heavy Duty line. New V-8s up to a whopping 534 cubic inches were offered, far outpowering the previous year's engines. GVWs rose to as much as 36,000 lbs on the F-Series, up to 51,000 lbs on the tandem-axle T-Series. Of more importance to tractor-trailer operators were Gross Combined Weight (GCW) ratings of 65,000 lbs with single rear axle, 75,000 with tandem axle.

1959

1959: Factory-built 4x4 pickups debut; Ford produces its 50-millionth car

Ranchero reflected the new look of Ford's ´59 car line, and gained two inches in wheelbase and a notable seven inches in cargo-bed length. Interiors were also redesigned. This restored example is powered by the base 223-cubic-inch six rated at 145 horsepower.

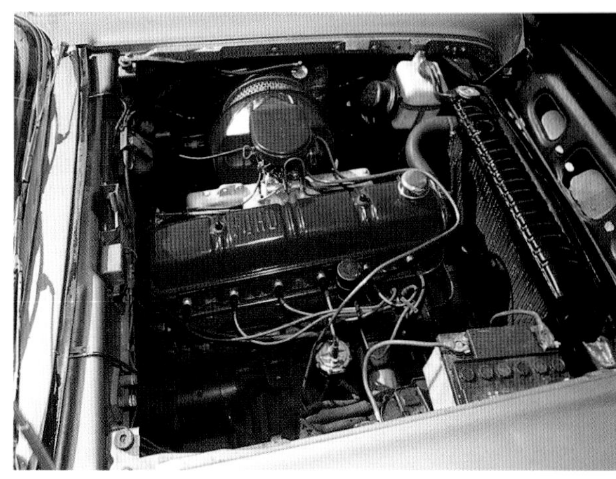

Go FORD-WARD for savings!

ALL-NEW CUSTOM RANCHERO! Longer wheelbase—7 inches more loadspace. Ranchero duplicates the luxury, the go, the smooth ride of a '59 Ford car . . . and it handles half-ton loads with ease! It's the most modern of all light trucks, *the prestige pickup for business.*

NEW TILT-CAB TANDEMS! Now, Ford tilt-cab tandems with ratings to 75,000 lbs. GCW! Now, all the advantages of tilt-cab design with the carrying capacity of tandems. Saves 3 ft. in length over all, provides greater payload capacity and saves hours of maintenance time!

2

3

4

5

1959

1. Though more buyers still chose the 6 ½-foot bed for their F-100s, the 8-foot bed was gaining in popularity and would eventually surpass its shorter sibling in sales. Likewise, the smooth-sided Styleside bed would soon top those of the "traditional" Flareside. 2. A Ford ad from 1959 touches on all the major advances that greeted truck buyers that year, including the F-Series' restyled grille, front bumper (now with carlike contours), and interior; the new 4-wheel-drive versions of the F-100 and F-250; the redesigned Ranchero; and tandem-axle versions of the popular C-Series. 3. Factory-built 4×4s, such as this F-250, would soon relegate the Marmon-Harrington conversions—which had been around since the Thirties—to history. 4. Topping the F-Series line for '59 were the F-1000 and F-1100. Note the hood scoop, which could be found on Super Duty F-Series trucks. 5. The C-Series saw few changes for 1959—and didn't need any. Tandem-axle versions were introduced in late 1958, which further increased their popularity.

Chapter Six: 1960-1969

Diesels, Economy Vans, and Bigger Trucks

1960-1969

Chapter Six

The Sixties will be remembered as a tumultuous time in our nation's history. For Ford Motor Company, however, it was a decade of exciting new product launches and expanded model offerings.

Two big events marked 1960; one the start of something small, the other an admission of failure. Introduced to great fanfare—and great success—was the compact Falcon, brought in to combat economy cars such as the Volkswagen Beetle. Though GM and Chrysler Corporation joined the fray at the same time with the Corvair and Valiant, the Falcon was the top seller of the three. Dismissed after a brief run of 1960 models was the ill-fated Edsel, a car that held a lot of promise upon introduction only to end its run as a failure of epic proportions.

Since the new Falcon line included a two-door station wagon, Ford took the opportunity to use it as the basis for a smaller, lighter Ranchero. Sales of the car/pickup crossover subsequently jumped from just over 14,000 for 1959 to more than 21,000 for 1960.

The success of the Ranchero was followed in 1961 by another Falcon derivative, the Econoline series. Also known as the E-Series, the line included a cargo van, a passenger van, and a pickup truck. The van was almost literally a box on wheels, with the pickup being a box with the top rear quarter removed.

Added to the opposite end of the truck spectrum for '61 was the heavy-duty H-Series. These trucks used modified Ford C-Series Tilt Cabs mounted high on the chassis, making them perfect for over-the-road, semi-tractor-trailer work.

Besides the new releases, Ford introduced a redesigned F-Series line for 1961 that featured new cabs, new front-end sheetmetal, and redesigned interiors. They were still offered in traditional Flareside (separate bed and fenders) and Styleside (smooth-sided bed) versions, but the Styleside was even smoother-sided than before, as the bed was made integral with the cab. Long a feature of the car-based Ranchero, it was something new for traditional pickups. However, the integrated cab and bed was only offered on two-wheel-drive models, as the company was evidently concerned about the increased twisting stress that might occur on 4×4s.

Because so much was new for '61, most trucks received only minor updates for '62. But the vacation didn't last long.

Ford opened the 1963 model year with the release of another new series of trucks. This line of medium- and heavy-duty models was referred to as the N-Series. Cabs were the same as those used for the F-Series, but the nose was significantly shorter. This arrangement placed the N-Series between Ford's conventional trucks and the C-Series Tilt Cabs, and made them popular for both city deliveries and over-the-road semi-tractor-trailer service where trailer-length limits were in force. In other heavy-duty news, Ford expanded diesel engine offerings to include some F-, C-, and N-Series trucks; previously, only the H-Series offered a diesel-engine option.

April 17, 1964, would go down in the annals of the Ford Motor Company as one of the company's best days, for it was on that day that Ford introduced the Mustang. Without question, it was the hit of the year, if not the decade.

On the truck side, 1964 brought a separate box for Styleside models, rendering the "unibody" pickups a thing of the past. Also new was a brace of gas engines for the medium- and heavy-duty lines.

Ford's famous Twin-I-Beam front suspension made news for 1965. It was offered only on light-duty two-wheel-drive F-Series trucks, giving them a softer ride and better handling characteristics.

For 1966, Ford once again introduced a new line of light-duty trucks as well as new heavy-duty line for over-the-road semi-tractor service. The former was a new four-wheel-drive sport-utility vehicle called the Bronco, which was offered in three body styles, all with either no top or one that could be removed. The latter were the flat-faced W-Series Cab-Over-Engine models, which would replaced the aging H-Series line. Also for '66, the Ranchero grew in size because the Falcon on which it was based was enlarged in a complete redesign.

Ford's F-Series trucks were restyled for the 1967 model year, though the extra-heavy-duty models still used the earlier 1961-1966 cab and front sheetmetal. New styling also graced the Ranchero, which took on the look of Ford's intermediate Fairlane.

New for 1968 was a redesigned Ranchero, again built off Ford's midsize car platform. Also, medium-duty trucks were offered with a diesel engine for the first time, but there were few other changes to any of the other truck lines.

Yet, one of Ford Motor Company's top stories for 1968 had nothing to do with any of its products. Newly installed as president was Semon E. "Bunkie" Knudsen, who had jumped ship from General Motors to lead crosstown rival Ford. This was a reversal of what had happened back in the early 1920s when Knudsen's father had left Ford to take over an ailing Chevrolet.

For 1969, the only noteworthy news was that the Econoline was redesigned for the first time since its 1961 introduction. It emerged much larger—and without its pickup derivative—and for the first time offered a V-8 option.

So as boisterous as Ford was through most of the Sixties, the company closed out the decade on a rather quiet note, with few other changes to either its car or truck lines. But that was only to save energy for the challenges that would face the company in the Seventies.

1960

1960: Redesigned Ranchero shrinks and goes unibody, being based on the new-for-1960 compact Falcon; Edsel discontinued

Ford conventionals entered the 1960s with carryover bodies but the traditional grille change; this year's extended down to the bumper and was joined by slots in the hood's leading edge. The restored F-100 pictured is powered by a 292-cubic-inch V-8 rated at 172 horsepower.

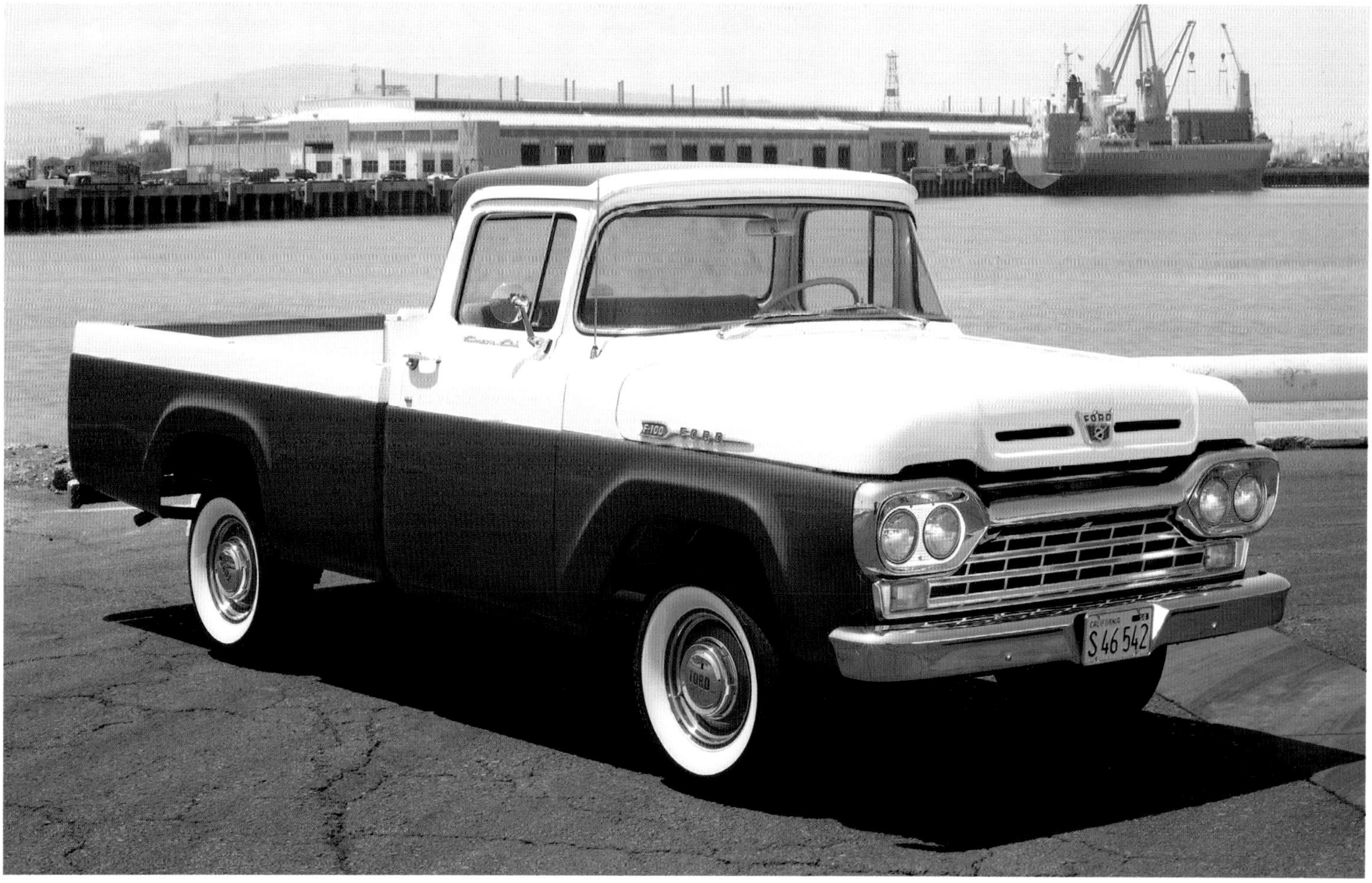

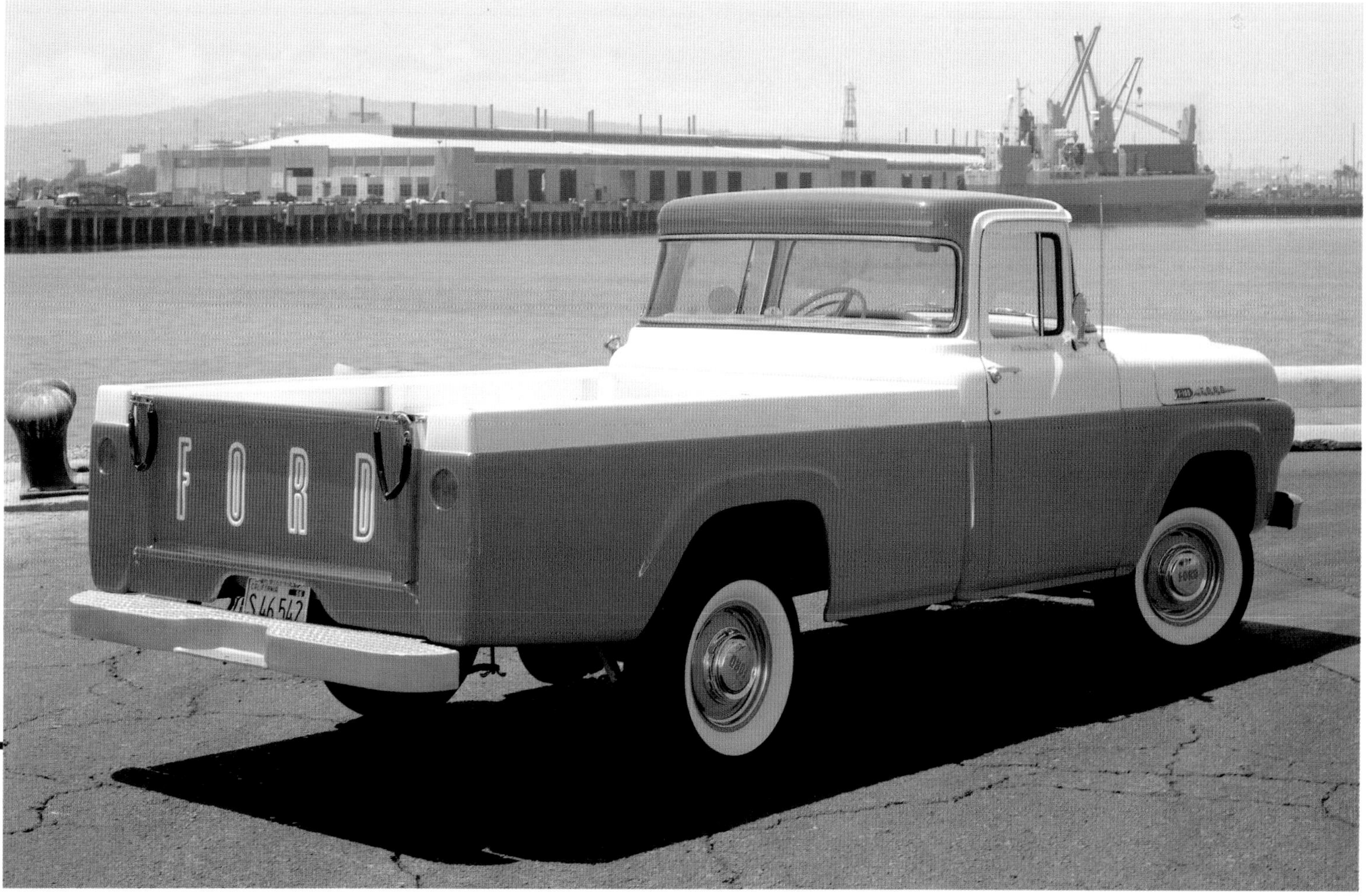

1960

1. The biggest news in Ford trucks for 1960 was the small Ranchero. Shifted from the full-size-car platform it had shared since its 1957 inception, Ranchero was now based on the compact Falcon, also new for 1960. In so doing, it lost its body-on-frame construction, adopting the Falcon's unibody design. Power came from a 144-cubic-inch six with 90 horsepower; a big step down from the beefy V-8s offered in its predecessor. Economy-minded buyers took note, and sales ran 50 percent ahead of the ′59 tally. 2. Intended for 1960, but delayed until ′61, was a Falcon-based Sedan Delivery—a prototype of which is shown here.

1

2

1. Ford pickups were again offered in four-wheel-drive form, as evidenced by this F-250. Though the "old style" Flareside bed with separate rear fenders was still offered, this vehicle's straight-sided Styleside bed was far more popular. 2-3. Trucks up to the F-600, shown here with a dump body, wore the 1960 light-duty models' grille, while F-700s and larger carried over the horizontal-bar ´59 design.

3

1961

1961: Most truck series redesigned; Econoline range introduced; diesel engines debut; Styleside pickup beds integrated with cab

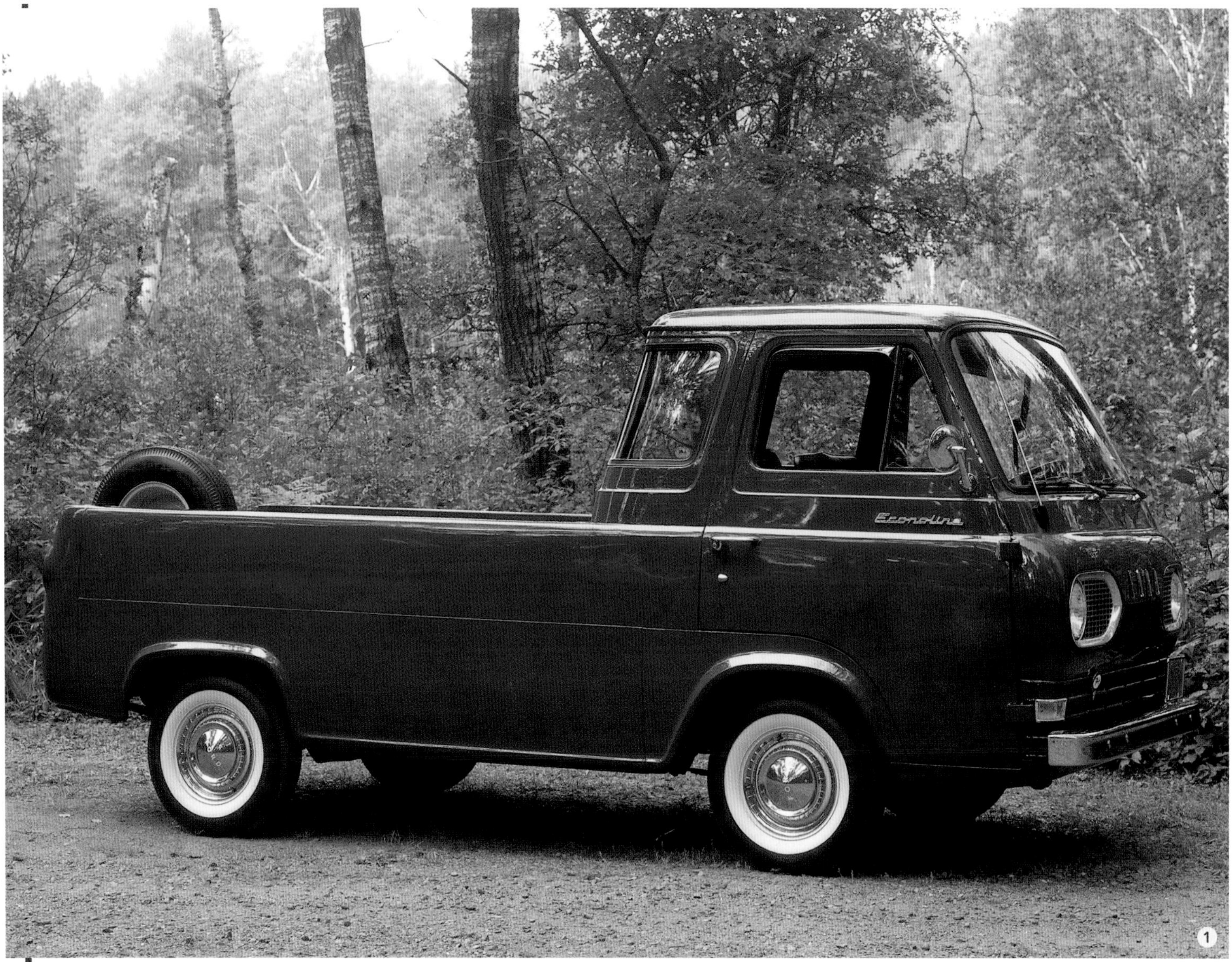

1

2

3

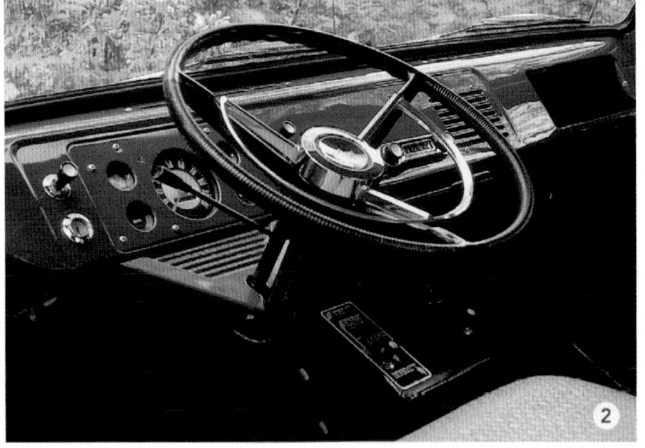

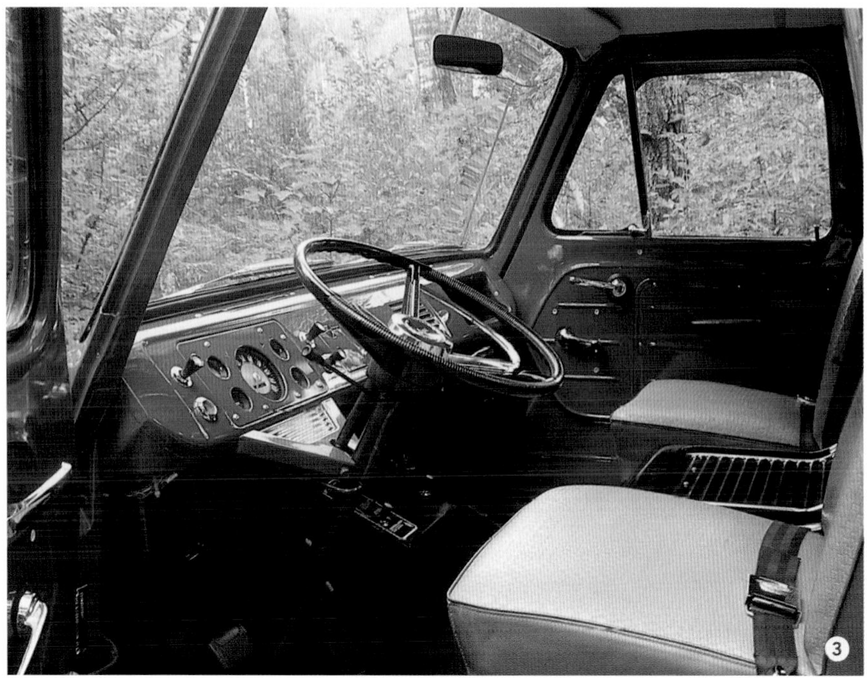

1-3. The new Falcon-based Econoline series included a short, forward-control pickup. Shown is the Deluxe version, which included rear quarter windows and extra chrome trim. The engine sat between the seats beneath a black cover. 4. Econolines were designated E-100, and in addition to a pickup, came in van and windowed passenger wagons. All were of modified unibody design, and powered by a 144-cubic-inch six rated at 85 horsepower. 5. Econoline pickups had a 7 ½-foot bed, placing them between the 6 ½- and eight-foot beds offered on the F-100, and cost about $85 less than the least-expensive F-100. The blanked-out quarter windows identify this as a base-trim model.

As shown on these F-100s, Styleside pickup beds were integrated with the cabs for 1961. Traditional Flareside beds continued to be offered as well, and both styles were available in 6 ½-and eight-foot lengths.

1. The P-Series Parcel Delivery, which hadn't received any significant changes since the early Fifties, continued that trend for 1961. 2. F-700s shared the front-end styling of lower F-Series models for 1961, whereas F-750s and up got a revised face. 3. C-Series trucks got dual headlights for '61 to replace the quad lights used since '58; in fact, they now looked nearly identical to the inaugural '57 models. Tandem rear axles and a GVW of up to 51,000 lbs mark this as a CT-950.

2

3

BROADER WARRANTIES...GREATER DURABILITY...BIGGER

'61 FORD SUPER DUTY TRUCKS

- New Super Duty V-8 Warranty—100,000 miles or 24 months!
- New extended warranty for entire truck—12 months or 12,000 miles!
- New stronger frames and huskier cabs for Conventional Cab models!
- Now 324 money-saving Super Duty models to choose from!

Now, durability with dollars behind it . . . the most liberal gasoline warranty ever offered! On 401-, 477- and 534-cu. in. engines, Ford dealers will replace every major engine part, including block, head, crankshaft, bearings, valves, pistons, rings found to be defective in material or workmanship, providing trucks are used in normal on-highway service. Warranty covers full cost of replacement parts for 100,000 miles or 24 months, whichever occurs first; full labor costs for first year or 50,000 miles, sliding percentage scale thereafter. In addition, an extended warranty covers the entire truck and is issued for all 1961 Ford Trucks. Each part, except tires and tubes, is now warranted by your dealer against defects in material and workmanship for 12 months or 12,000 miles, whichever comes first. The warranty does not apply, of course, to normal maintenance service or to the replacement in normal maintenance of parts such as filters, spark plugs, and ignition points. Never before have you had such protection for your truck investment; never could you be so confident of long-range economy!

102 ALL-NEW H-SERIES TILT CAB MODELS

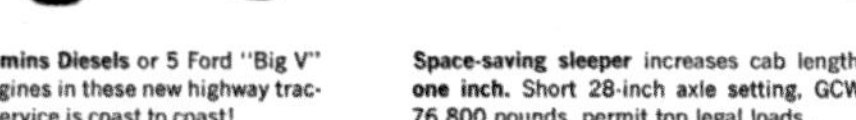

5 Cummins Diesels or 5 Ford "Big V" gas engines in these new highway tractors. Service is coast to coast!

Space-saving sleeper increases cab length by only **one inch.** Short 28-inch axle setting, GCW's up to 76,800 pounds, permit top legal loads.

107 C-SERIES TILT CAB MODELS WITH NEW

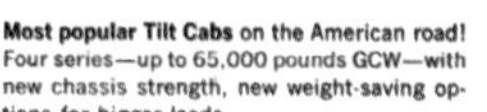

Most popular Tilt Cabs on the American road! Four series—up to 65,000 pounds GCW—with new chassis strength, new weight-saving options for bigger loads.

New compact sleeper adds only 2½ inches to cab length, lets you haul 40-foot trailers in 50-foot states. Wide range of optional tractor equipment available on all models.

115 NEW HIGH-STRENGTH CONVENTIONAL

New huskier tractors feature lighter, stronger frames of high-tensile steel . . . heavier gauge metal and stress-isolating mounting for cabs. New 28-in. BA for extra payload!

New tougher tandems offer new strength in chassis, cab sheet metal . . . new shock-swallowing front suspension. Powered by rugged "Big V" engines, Ford tandems range up to 51,000 lbs. GVW, 75,000 GCW.

1

2

3

CE !

AND GAS!

d is big advantage of new, " tandem axles. Over 500 combinations, all told!

R OPTION!

re also available in the tional tandems, aluminum nd fuel tanks are offered to d.

DELS!

D
CKS
T
S

1961

4

5

1. Ford's Super Duty line expanded in '61 with the addition of the H-Series, which featured a taller tilt cab than the C-Series. H's were also available with the first diesel engines offered in a Ford truck, all built by Cummins. The main photo depicts a red Super Duty conventional, which started at the F-750 level and featured a different front-end design than lighter-duty conventionals. 2-3. Replacing the full-size Courier car-based delivery vehicle for 1961 was a new Falcon-based Sedan Delivery. Unlike its Courier predecessor, the new model featured "proper" blanked-out rear side windows. 4. A number of companies—including Ford—built the Willys-designed M151 MUTT (Mobile Utility Tactical Truck) military vehicle starting in the early Sixties. Unlike the contemporary civilian Jeep CJ, they were of unit construction with four-wheel independent suspension. The M151 was soon updated with a heavier-duty rear suspension to become the M151A1. 5. A six-cylinder engine had been absent from the medium-duty line for a few years when Ford brought one back for 1961. The reason was better mileage: Ads claimed the 262-cubic-inch, 152-horsepower engine got "8% better gas economy than Ford's principal competitor..."—meaning Chevrolet. 6. Ranchero returned with few changes for '61 except for the optional availability of a 170-cubic-inch six to replace the standard 144-cid unit.

6

1962

1962: Ranchero and Sedan Delivery facelifted; Econoline passenger wagon becomes a Falcon model; F-Series Styleside models begin reverting back to separate cab/bed design

3

1. Ranchero greeted 1962 with a fresh face that included a new flush-mounted grille and pointed front fenders, but little else changed. 2. The Sedan Delivery likewise sported the new look, but also saw few other alterations. 3. Econoline's biggest change for '61 was in name only. The passenger version, formerly referred to as the Station Bus, was now called a Falcon and considered a car. Newly optional was a 170-cubic-inch six.

4

4. Ford had entered the diesel market in 1961 with Cummins-powered versions of the H-Series high tilt cab, designated the HD-Series. This HD-1000 came equipped with the largest of these engines, displacing 743 cubic inches and rated at 220 horsepower. 5-6. F-Series grilles were slightly revised for 1962, replacing the FORD lettering in the middle with cross bars. Also for '62, Styleside 4×4s (5) came with a separate cab/bed, unlike the integrated bed on 4×2 models (6)—though the latter would offer the separate cab/bed midyear.

5

6

1963

1963: N-Series short conventional introduced; diesel power newly offered on several medium- and heavy-duty models; top diesel engine now a Cummins 265-horsepower V-8; one-ton version of E-Series debuts; V-8 made available in Ranchero and Sedan Delivery midyear.

1-4. E-100 pickups and cargo vans retained the Econoline moniker after the passenger wagon was renamed "Falcon" in ′61. Newly available on Econolines was a one-ton payload package.
5-6. In addition to a new crosshatch grille for ′63, Rancheros and Sedan Deliverys were blessed with an optional V-8 at midyear.

FORD
1963
4

1963
5

6

1963

1-2. F-Series trucks got a new grille for ´63 but were otherwise little-changed. All 4×4s again had a separate cab and bed. 3-5. Rear-drive F-100s were offered with three different bed designs: a separate Styleside; a traditional Flareside; and a Styleside integrated with the cab, a version that would be dropped after ´63. 6. Ford supplied chassis and powertrains to the growing motorhome industry during the 1960s. Note the grille, which is similar to that used on contemporary Ford N-Series trucks. 7. The 500- and 600-series trucks were considered medium-duty rigs. An F-600 is shown here with the traditional Stake Bed body.

1

2

3

4

F O R D
100
1963
F O R D
F O R D
600
1963

1963

Ford's Super duty line is represented here by an H-Series high tilt cab (1), F-Series conventional (2), and a new-for-'63 N-Series short conventional (3). The H and N carry diesel engines, as indicated by the nose badge on the H and the nose lettering on the N.

1964

1964: Ranchero redesigned; new double-walled bed for F-Series pickups; new series of gas engines for medium- and heavy-duty trucks; air conditioning optional on select models

1. Ford offered a wide selection of light-duty trucks in the Sixties, though they were matched one-for-one by rival Chevrolet. The biggest news for ′64 was the redesigned Ranchero (front row, center), which was again based on the likewise redesigned Falcon compact car. 2. Grilles changed a bit on the popular F-Series, as shown on this F-250 4×4, which sports an eight-foot Flareside bed.

1964

1. A splashy, three-page ad touts the virtues of Ford's 1964 F-Series pickups and E-Series vans. The pickup's Styleside bed featured a double-wall design, which prevented shifting cargo from denting the outside sheetmetal, and a central release lever for the tailgate. Econoline vans could be fitted with both right- and left-side cargo doors for '64, and a Heavy-Duty version was available that upped payload capacity from 1650 lbs to 2000. 2. By 1964, an F-Series pickup could be fitted with such carlike features as two-tone paint and air conditioning. 3. Ford's 600-800 series trucks were powered by new V-8 engines for '64. Essentially heavy-duty versions of their automotive counterparts, they displaced 330, 361, and 391 cubic inches, with 186 to 235 horsepower. 4. An E-100 was set up as a mobile service station—complete with actual gas pump—by Raymond C. Dietz, of Borger, Texas.

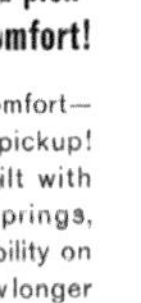

d pick-
mfort!

mfort—
pickup!
ilt with
prings,
oility on
v longer
gs that
noother
of cab
e yet!

00,000-
pendent
r gravel
100,000
issions,
l. Total
tenance
per mile!

Easier ride with a new longer wheelbase. New 128-inch wheelbase is longer than that of many luxury cars . . . gives you a smoother, more relaxing ride on any road surface.

Easier loading with a new one-hand tailgate. Single handle in center operates spring catches at ends of tailgate on new Styleside models. Opens, closes with one hand!

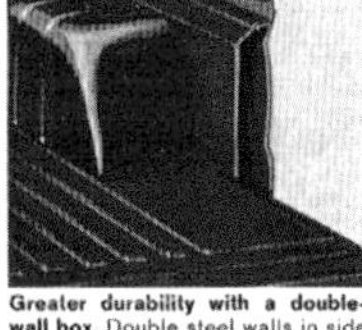

Greater durability with a double-wall box. Double steel walls in side panels of new boxes—sleeker on the outside, stronger on the inside. Tailgate holds 2,000 lbs!

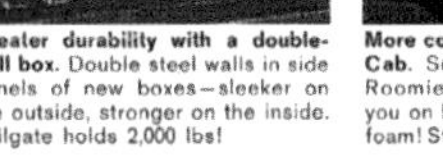

More comfort with a new Driverized Cab. Smart as a station wagon! Roomier new Custom Cab seats you on 5 full inches of comfortable foam! Storage compartment in door!

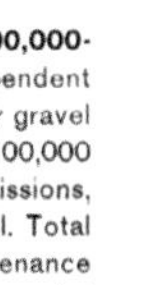

2 to 1
erate!

, in just
ry truck.
antages:
han old-
to eight
w price
missions,
d capa-
s in '64!

s...2.7
mile test
showed
Econo-
preven-
ed only
te, certi-
!

More payload with 1-ton capacity. New optional heavy-duty model increases payload from 1,650 lbs. to 2,000 lbs.—opens the way to new uses for versatile Econoline Vans!

Surer stopping with new self-adjusting brakes. Brakes automatically adjust themselves, increase safety . . . . reduce shop time. New, thicker linings last up to 37% longer!

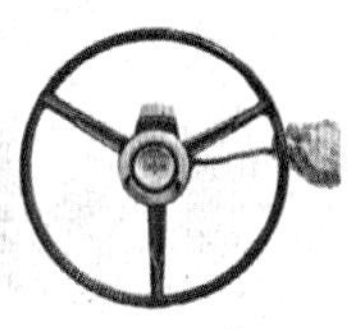

Better performance with new transmissions. Optional automatic and 4-speed traffic transmissions enable you to "tailor" your drive line for top performance and economy!

More convenience with long, low flat floor. Low level floor—only knee-high and with no rear engine hump—lets you slide heavy loads straight through from rear to front!

Avenue, Chicago, Illinois 60611. Second-class postage paid at Chicago, Ill. and at additional mailing offices

MORE FOR '64

MORE LOADSPACE

Ford's Econoline Van gives you up to 56 percent more loadspace than old-style panels. This can mean only two trips instead of three to haul the same load! Cargo floor is flat, front to rear, with no space-stealing rear engine hump to interfere with long loads.

REGULAR 1,650-LB. CAPACITY

NEW OPTIONAL 2,000-LB. CAPACITY

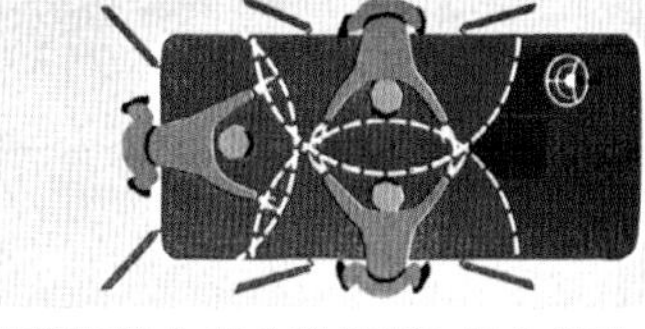

MORE WEIGHT CAPACITY

Now you can choose either the standard Econoline with a capacity of 1,650 lbs., or the new Heavy-Duty Econoline that hauls 2,000 lbs.! Options include automatic and 4-speed traffic transmissions, storage bins!

MORE LOADING EASE

No longer must you sort your load to a time-consuming "first on, last off" plan. With up to 8 big doors for easy access, every part of your load is always right at hand—at every stop you make! Saves time, work every trip.

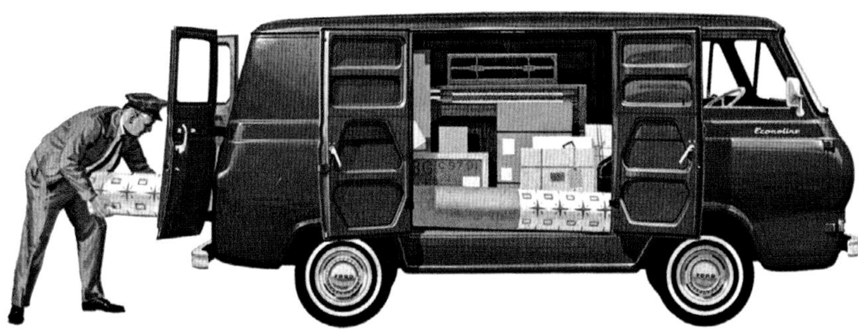

MORE THAN 100,000 SATISFIED OWNERS

In just three short years Econoline has become America's most popular delivery truck—over 100,000 pleased owners have proved its outstanding durability and economy! More proof comes from an independent research firm. They ran two '63 Econoline trucks night and day for 100,000 miles each. Total operating costs for this run—gas, oil, tires, preventive maintenance and repairs—averaged only 2.7 cents per mile! No wonder Econoline outsells other vans 2 to 1! See your Ford Dealer now for a '64 Econoline!

4

1965

1965: Twin-I-Beam front suspension offered on pickups; new six-cylinder and V-8 engines debut; extended-length Econoline introduced

1

1. Twin-I-Beam independent front suspension was made standard on F-100 and F-250 4×2s for 1965. The advancement in ride comfort took top billing in this ad, which also mentioned the F-Series' new six-cylinder engines (measuring 240 and 300 cubic inches), and its new 352-cid V-8. 2-5. Equipped with the 352 V-8 and automatic transmission, this restored F-100 looks quite flashy with its whitewall tires, chrome trim, and two-tone paint scheme—inside and out. The dashboard was redesigned for ’65.

2

3

4

5

1965

1. A Camper Special package offered in 1965 was aimed at the growing number of buyers who wanted to carry their homes on their backs while vacationing. It included heavy-duty radiator and battery, dual extended mirrors, and extra gauges. 2. Rancheros could also get "Deluxe" trim, in this case called the Futura Ornamentation Package. 3. The Deluxe Club Wagon version of the Falcon included bright bodyside trim and chrome bumpers outside, and padded instrument panel and pleated vinyl seats inside. The rear bumper was redesigned for ′65 to be interchangeable with the front. Cargo versions sold under the Econoline name added a SuperVan version that added 18 inches between the rear wheel and bumper, which in turn added nearly 25 percent to its cargo capacity. 4. Highest-rated capacity of all Ford trucks for ′65 was the T-950, with a GVW of up to 78,000 lbs. Shown is a version equipped with a Cummins diesel engine, making it a T-950-D. 5. Though equipped with a sleeper cab, this C-750 didn't seem to offer much room to lie down. Both gas and diesel versions were offered.

1966

1966: Bronco sport-utility vehicle debuts; Ranchero redesigned on midsize car platform; H-Series high tilt cab succeeded by W-Series; SuperVan version of Falcon passenger wagon introduced

Aimed squarely at the Jeep CJ and International Scout, Ford's Bronco arrived for 1966 in three body styles, all with four-wheel drive. Shown is the Wagon version, which could seat up to four. Its metal top (painted white) could be removed and the windshield could be folded down, thus enabling the Bronco to be turned into a truly "open" vehicle. A 170-cubic-inch six was standard, but a 289-cid V-8 was added as an option later in the model year.

1966

1. Least expensive of the Broncos was the Roadster, which came with no doors or top. A U-shaped fiberglass panel was fitted to the door opening to round the edges and provide a more "finished" look. 2. The Sports Utility version was a two-seater with a very short pickup bed. Like the Wagon, its top could be removed and windshield folded. 3. Interiors showed a bit of flare for what was a rather utilitarian vehicle. 4. A Sports Utility with camper was perfect for those yearning to vacation in out-of-the-way places.

1-2. The Falcon line moved to larger bodies for 1966, and the Falcon-based Ranchero followed suit. In so doing, it gained nearly four inches in wheelbase and eight inches in length. Options included a 225-horsepower 289-cubic-inch V-8 and four-speed manual transmission. 3-4. A restyled grille was the only change of note to the ´66 F-series pickups. This restored example boasts upscale Custom Cab trim.

1. A crew-cab body for the F-Series became available in 1965; it was little-changed for ′66. F-250 crews offered a six-foot bed, F-350s—as pictured here—an eight-foot bed. Note that the bed dates from the 1957-63 generation of F-Series pickups. 2. Another older-style bed used for 1966 was the nine-footer offered on the F-350. 3. The H-Series high tilt cab was replaced by the flat-faced W-Series in mid 1966. All Ws were diesel powered, with a wide choice of engines from Caterpillar, Cummins, and Detroit Diesel. 4. F-350s fitted with a wrecker body were popular for tow truck use.

1

2

1966

3

4

1967

1967: F-Series redesigned; Ranchero shifted to Fairlane body

1-2. A 1967 F-Series restyle brought a pronounced side spear and cleaner front-end appearance. Interiors were redesigned along with the exteriors, getting a more carlike instrument panel. 3. This time, crew cabs got a bed that matched the lines of the cab and front fenders.

1967

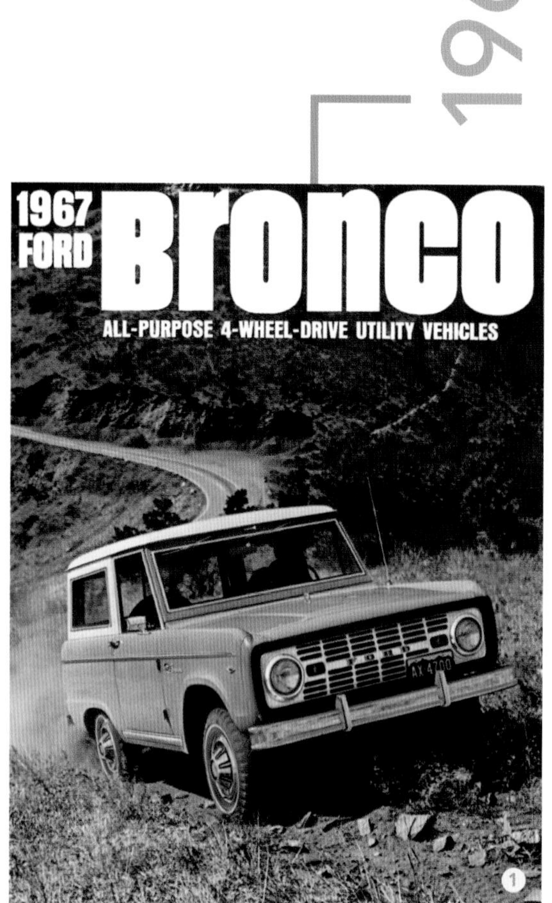

1-2. Bronco returned for 1967 with few changes, though the Sport Utility was renamed the Pickup. 3. While similar from the windshield back to the 1966 version, the ´67 Ranchero sported the front styling of the Fairlane rather than the Falcon, which brought vertically stacked headlights. Newly optional was Ford's 390-cubic-inch V-8 with up to 320 horsepower.

1. Medium-duty trucks adopted the cab and hood of the redesigned 1967 light-duty pickups, but got flared front fenders to accommodate a wider track, as shown on this F-600 Stake Bed. 2. Few changes marked the ’67 W-Series, represented here by a W-1000-D. Actually, the "-D" wasn't really needed to denote "Diesel," as all W-Series trucks were oil-burners.

1968

1968: Ranchero redesigned; medium-duty trucks get available diesel V-8

1

1. Ford's midsize-car line was redesigned for 1968, and with it, the car-based Ranchero. The top engine was initially a 390-cubic-inch V-8, but added as a midyear option was Ford's mighty 428 Cobra Jet. 2. F-Series pickups got slight grille revisions for '68, along with federally mandated side marker lights; they were integrated with the badge at the top of the fender in front, and on the lower fender in back. Also new that year were optional 360- and 390-cubic-inch V-8s and fully integrated air conditioning. 3-5. Aside from the addition of side marker lights, Bronco continued into 1968 with only minor changes in carryover Wagon, Pickup, and Roadster body styles.

2

3

4

5

1969: Econoline redesigned to be much larger and offer V-8 power; new truck engines debut; Bronco Roadster discontinued

A new Econoline appeared for 1969 that was significantly larger, came in two wheelbases, and offered a 302-cubic-inch V-8 as an option. However, the line lacked a pickup version, and vans could no longer be ordered with a left-side cargo door. The engine was moved forward, and fluids could be checked by opening the short hood. Ford's Twin-I-Beam front suspension was standard. Both versions pictured sit on the longer wheelbase.

1969

1969

1

1. The military MUTT (Mobile Utility Tactical Truck) built by Ford and other companies starting in the early Sixties was revised in 1969 in an effort to cure a handling problem that made them unstable in quick changes of direction. Designated the M151A2, these vehicles could be easily identified by their one-piece windshield. The MUTT would be replaced by the Hummer in the early 1980s after a 20-year run. 2. The sporty Ranchero GT came with a hood scoop and a bodyside C-stripe that was revised for 1969. Also offered were styled steel wheels. Base GT engine was a 302-cubic-inch V-8, but a new 351 was available, along with carryover 390- and 428-cid options. 3. A Contractors Special package was offered on F-Series pickups that included side boxes for the bed and an optional underhood 110-volt generator. F-Series grilles were changed only slightly for ’69. 4. Due to their large interior volume, E-Series vans were popular for ambulance conversions. 5. A C-Series forward-control truck looked nearly the same in 1969 as it did in debut 1957. Its set-back front axle gave it a tight turning radius that made it particularly well-suited for urban-delivery use.

3

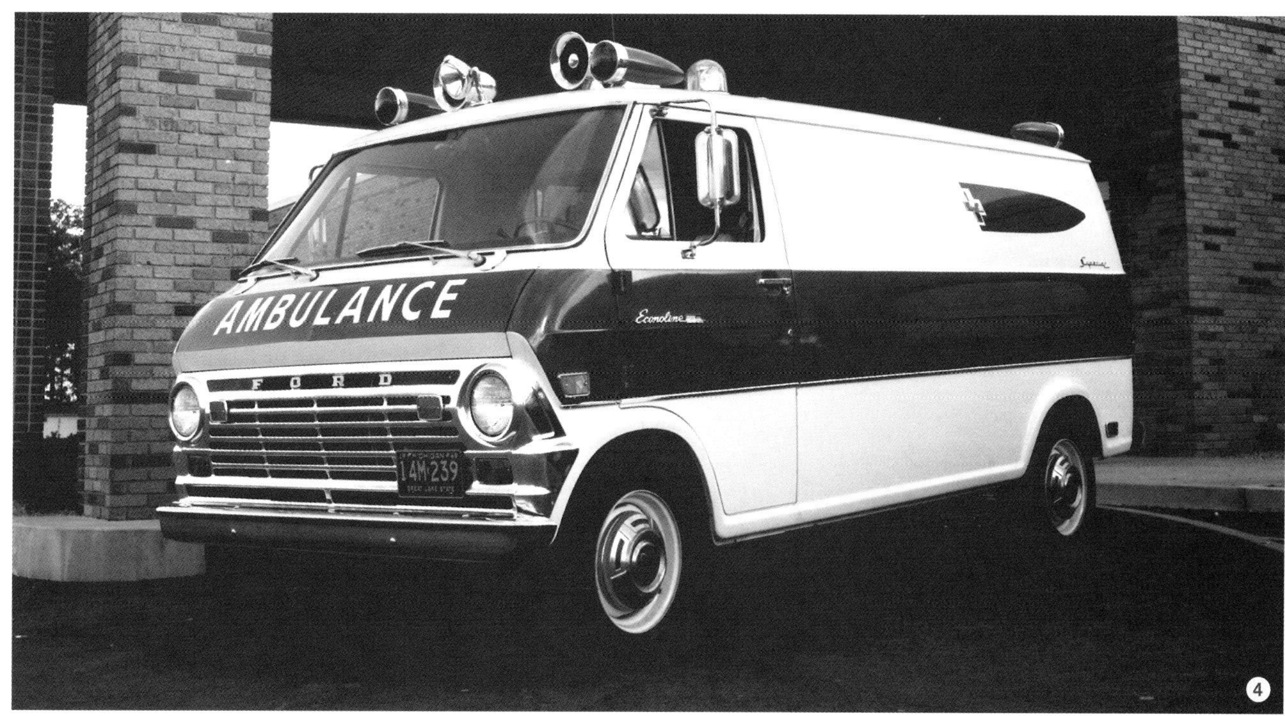

4

5

For car enthusiasts, the 1970s could best be described as the "Forgettable Decade." Government-mandated safety, emissions, and fuel-economy standards hit automakers with a triple whammy, forcing them to rethink strategies that had served them well in the Sixties. "Performance" became a dirty word, bigger was no longer better, and styling was often sacrificed to safety. As a result, very few cars excited the senses.

Not so, however, in the world of trucks. Since many of the government standards either didn't apply to trucks or weren't as strict, these beasts of burden didn't fall prey to the forces that beleaguered their automotive brethren. Which might be one reason trucks gained so much in popularity over the decade.

Ford greeted the Seventies by opening a new truck plant near Louisville, Kentucky. Though it was officially called the Kentucky Truck Plant, it was quickly dubbed the "Louisville Plant" because its main claim to fame was as the point of assembly for Ford's new Louisville Line, also known as the L-Series. These heavy-duty trucks replaced the short conventional N-Series, along with the bigger F-Series and related tandem-axle T-Series. The Louisville Line thus encompassed a wide range of models serving the medium-, heavy-, and extra-heavy-duty ranks, and would go on to become one of the most popular series of trucks Ford ever produced.

About the only other news for 1970 was a redesigned Ranchero, which adopted the look of Ford's new midsize car line, which added a Torino derivative. Ranchero GT got Laser Stripe side decoration, while a new Squire model replaced that with a woodgrain appliqué.

Chapter Seven: 1970-1979

A Louisville Line and a Courier, Too

1970-1979

Chapter Seven

Other than minor trim updates, the 1971 lineup was little-changed from 1970, Ford concentrating instead on its new subcompact Pinto and a redesigned Mustang.

Ranchero underwent another update for ´72, but that wasn't the biggest truck news that year. No, the biggest news was something small: the Courier. Supplied by Mazda of Japan, the Courier was a compact pickup with a four-cylinder engine, intended to compete against the increasingly popular small pickups from Toyota and Nissan.

Nineteen seventy-three brought a redesign for the F-Series, which included longer cabs and restyled exterior body panels. Ford also took this opportunity to update the extra-heavy-duty Cab-Over-Engine (COE) W-Series by rounding its corners to make it more aerodynamic. And Ranchero got a restyled front end incorporating the five-mph bumper mandated that year for its automotive counterparts.

But perhaps the biggest news of 1973 didn't come out of a Ford plant. In October of that year, the Oil Producing Export Countries, thereafter better known as OPEC, restricted the flow of oil to the U.S., thus triggering America's first energy crisis. This would end up having far-reaching effects that went well beyond simply boosting the price of gas, as it prompted the government to enact Corporate Average Fuel Economy (CAFE) standards for vehicles that remain in effect today.

While most of Ford's focus was on a smaller new Mustang for 1974, trucks were not completely ignored. New for the F-Series that year was its first extended cab, which allowed buyers to carry extra passengers or more cargo inside the cab.

It was the Econoline's turn to shine for 1975, sporting its first redesign since growing larger in 1968. But what would turn out to be an even bigger event—though it was hardly that at the time—was the introduction of a "heavy ½-ton" F-Series. Called the F-150, it was intended to be a gap-filler between the F-100 and F-250. But what it ended up being was the first of what would eventually become America's most popular vehicle.

Customized vans were trendy back in the mid 1970s, and Ford decided to cash in on this youth-market phenomenon by introducing some factory-customized models for 1976. Ford basically did what a private owner might do: add custom wheels and exterior decoration, and upgrade the interior with fancier seats and trim. Ford called these custom Econolines Cruising Vans, a very appropriate title.

On the large side of the truck ledger, Ford also offered a new Louisville model called the LTL-9000. This new premium model was basically a long-nosed version of the regular L-Series truck.

Nineteen seventy-seven marked Ford's 60th year in the trucking business, and the company made no attempt to hide that fact in advertising. Ranchero and Courier were updated, and dress-up packages influenced by the success of the Cruising Van were offered on some other truck lines. And at the end of the 1977 model year, Ford's F-Series pickup was christened the number-one-selling vehicle in the United States.

Bronco underwent a major redesign in 1978, the first since its 1966 introduction. The new version was substantially larger, heavier, and better-equipped than its predecessor, and proved more popular—by a wide margin.

This was also the year Ford brought out a successor to the W-Series extra-heavy-duty trucks. These new Fords carried the CL-9000 designation and represented quite an improvement over the models they replaced. Ford also celebrated its 75th Anniversary and made a special note of reaching that mark through a very successful national sales promotion campaign.

Nineteen seventy-nine brought a new promotional campaign for trucks: the famous "Built Ford Tough" slogan. It would also mark the end of the Ranchero, whose sales had dropped off in recent years.

But a far more historically significant occurrence of 1979 was our nation's second oil crisis, again triggered by events in the Middle East. In many ways it was worse than the first, with sharply higher gas prices being exacerbated by rationing in some areas. So far-reaching were its effects that it triggered a serious economic recession, and would profoundly influence the design of vehicles for many years to come.

1970

1970: Louisville—or L-Line—conventional heavy- and extra-heavy-duties debut; car-based Ranchero pickup is thoroughly restyled

An all-new styling theme for the Torino family of midsize cars also translated into new looks for the Ranchero pickup. Pointed front-fender tips, a sharp full-length midbody crease, and an eggcrate grille were key elements of the new design, though hidden headlamps were an extra-cost option. Base, 500, and GT Rancheros were continued from before, but the Squire—generously decked out in simulated wood trim—was new to the line. A trio of 429-cubic-inch V-8s now topped the engine roster in place of 390- and 428-cid mills.

1-2. The gradual push toward comfort and luxury in light trucks gained added momentum at Ford with the arrival of Ranger XLT trim for certain F-Series models. XLT equipment bested Ranger gear with items like a woodgrained tailgate appliqué, full-length lower-body moldings, cloth-and-vinyl upholstery, carpeting, and other conveniences. This F-100 Ranger XLT also sports an extra-cost vinyl roof covering. 3. An F-Series Ranger with four-wheel drive rode high off the ground. A chrome front bumper was newly standard on pickups.

1970

1. A new L-Line truck family replaced the N-, T-, and largest F-Series models. The LNT-800 was the lighter of two gas-engine, "short-nose" tandem-axle models. 2. LTs had a foot-longer hood than LNTs. Diesel engine options were expanded in the new L-Line. 3. A late addition to the line was the LTS, marked by its setback front axle. It was popular for construction work. 4. The heavy-duty gas-powered C-900 version of the Tilt Cab was revived after 11 years.

1971

1971: Changes are minimal throughout Ford's truck offerings; special-order crew cab availability expanded to F-700, -7000, and -750

Among the more substantial improvements made in the 1971 Ford truck family was the new heavy-duty axle fitted to Bronco sport-utility vehicles. The 12.7-gallon fuel tank, first used only on '70 models with evaporative emissions-recovery systems, was another new across-the-board addition, and front bucket seats were standardized during the model year.

1971

1. A group portrait of Ford's 1971 light-duty truck family includes, clockwise from left, a Bronco sport-utility, a long-wheelbase Econoline Club Wagon, the bread-and-butter F-Series pickup (here an F-250 Camper Special), and a sporty Ranchero GT. 2. Econolines got a new grille, and the 240-cubic-inch six was standard in all models. 3. A nicer interior was among the changes made to W-Series tractors. 4. The LTS's setback front axle allowed it to carry a greater percentage of the total load in addition to providing a tighter turning radius.

3

1972

1972: Ranchero redesigned; Club Wagons and Econolines adopt sliding side doors in place of side-hinged doors; Bronco pickup is produced for the last time; engine horsepower now measured in net rather than gross ratings; Mazda-built Courier compact pickup announced in March

1

1. Until the Courier started coming over from Mazda in Japan that spring, Ford's smallest and lightest truck offerings for 1972 were the wholly redesigned Ranchero and the carryover Bronco. Beneath its all-new sheetmetal, the Ranchero—available in three trim levels—gained four inches in wheelbase (to 118) and was of a body-on-frame design for the first time since 1959. The coil-spring rear suspension was revised, too. Engine choices included a 250-cubic-inch six and five V-8s ranging from 302 to 429 cid. 2-4. Broncos with the Sport option package featured bright trim inside and out, plus fancier upholstery. All Broncos got bigger brakes in '72. With tightening exhaust-emissions standards, the 302-cid V-8 became the base engine for California-bound Broncos, though the 170-cid six was still available there as a special-order item.

1972

1. The Econoline Camper Special was in its first full model year, having been introduced partway through 1971. Built on the E-300 Super Van Cutaway chassis, it came with a 302-cubic-inch V-8 and automatic transmission as standard equipment. 2-3. The extremes of the ½-ton F-100 range: a full-dress Explorer with lots of bright trim and coloful upholstery, and an all-business entry-level Custom. 4. Four-wheel-drive F-250s got a beefier Spicer front axle for '72. 5. An F-250 Camper Special was offered on the crew cab chassis-and-cab platform. 6. The W-Series remained Ford's "big dog." New Owner-Operator option groups with comfort and appearance features were created to appeal to independent truckers.

FORD
6

1973

1973: F-Series light- and medium-duties get roomier new cabs in first full redo since 1967; over-the-road W-Series updated at midyear with sleeker cab contours, L-Line-inspired radiator grille, and other detail changes

1. Ford's domestically built light trucks for 1973 included, clockwise from left, the Bronco, F-100, and Ranchero. The Bronco carried on in much the same form as it had since its 1966 introduction, but the F-100 had an all-new cab design and front sheetmetal, while the Ranchero featured a frontal facelift and—thanks to its passenger-car ties—an energy-absorbing front bumper. 2. The 1973 Ranchero GT featured a new bodyside striping design, plus white-letter tires (in place of whitewalls) as standard equipment. Body-color racing mirrors, high-back bucket seats, and a 140-horsepower 302-cubic-inch V-8 were other basic features of this sportiest of the three Ranchero models.

1

2

1. When the limited-edition Explorer pickups returned for 1973, lower-body striping was a new addition to the package. 2. The new F-Series cab design incorporated behind-the-seat storage for incidental items. 3. The Ranger trim package for Broncos added fancy appointments inside and out, plus an external swing-away spare-tire carrier. The 200-cubic-inch six became the new base powerplant for Broncos.

3

1973

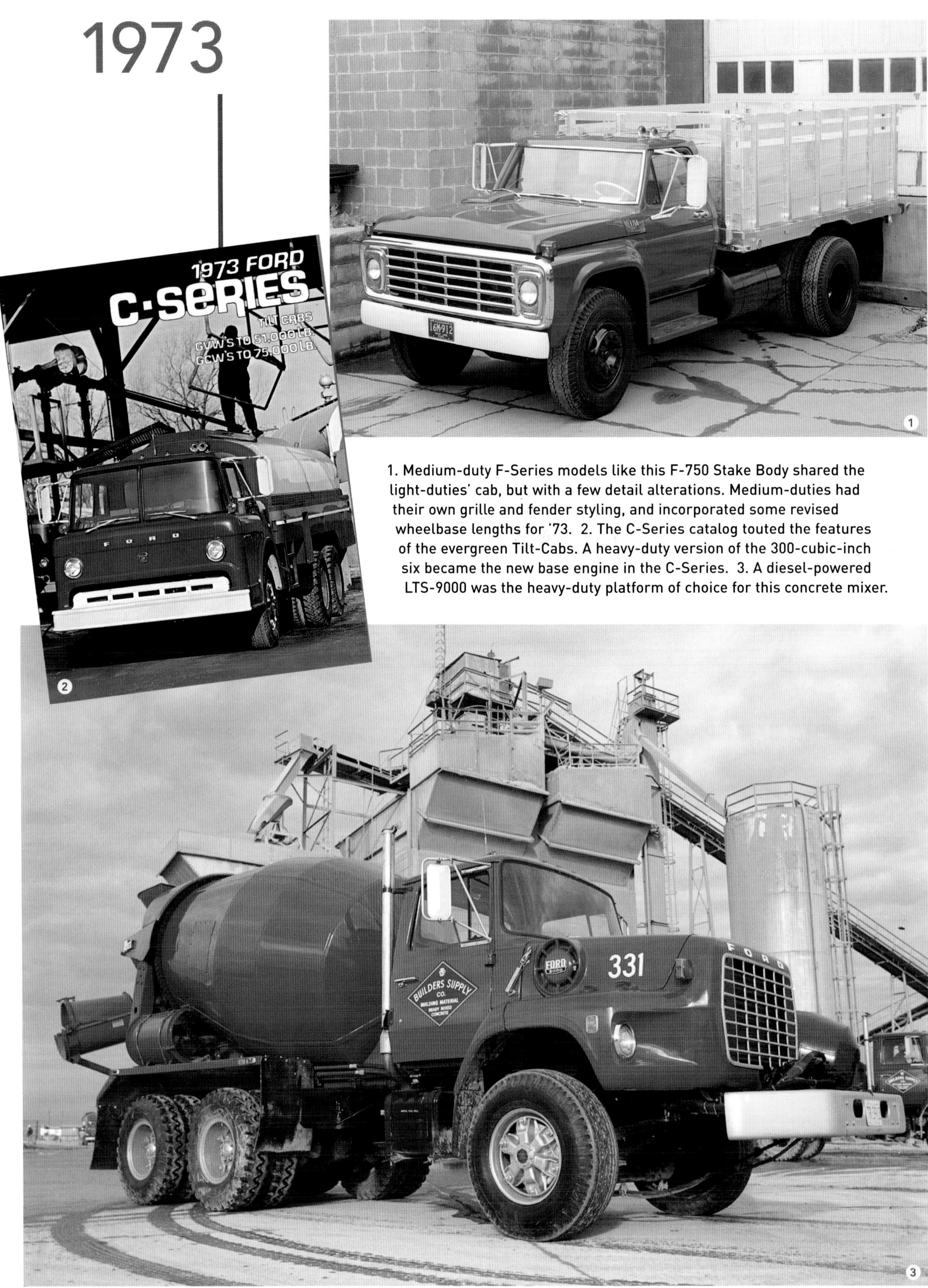

1. Medium-duty F-Series models like this F-750 Stake Body shared the light-duties' cab, but with a few detail alterations. Medium-duties had their own grille and fender styling, and incorporated some revised wheelbase lengths for '73. 2. The C-Series catalog touted the features of the evergreen Tilt-Cabs. A heavy-duty version of the 300-cubic-inch six became the new base engine in the C-Series. 3. A diesel-powered LTS-9000 was the heavy-duty platform of choice for this concrete mixer.

1974: Following Dodge's lead, Ford adds SuperCab pickups to F-Series line with added interior space for cargo or second-row passengers; full-time four-wheel drive becomes an option for some light-duty pickups; Ranchero goes all V-8 at the worst-possible time—the beginning of the 1973-74 oil crisis—but reinstates base six by April '74; new wider fenders on tried-and-true C-Series Tilt Cabs

1. Ford responded to Dodge's pioneering 1973 extended-cab pickup with the SuperCab, which joined the F-Series roster in June 1974. The 22-inch-long extension was large enough to accommodate an optional forward-facing bench or side-facing jump seats. 2. Now that there were two kinds, "conventional" pickups became known as regular cabs. F-Series styling was carried over unchanged from '73.

1974

1-2. Recreational-vehicle alternatives from '74 on one-ton chassis included an Econoline E-300 Camper Special with an integral motor home body, and an F-350 Super Camper Special with a removable camper unit. 3. A sliding door remained an option in place of dual side-hinged doors on cargo vans. SuperVans with the extra-cost Custom Equipment Package and wheel covers delivered utility with style and comfort. 4. Nineteen seventy-four marked the last year the original Bronco would be offered with a six-cylinder engine.

1975

1975: Third generation of Econoline vans and wagons arrives; F-150 makes debut in light-duty pickup line

1. A bigger, brawnier Econoline family was launched for 1975. Mounted on a separate frame for the first time ever, new E-Series vehicles were available on longer wheelbases of 124 and 138 inches. Gross vehicle weights rose across the board, too, which showed in new nomenclature. The E-100 was joined by the E-250, E-350, and an all-new E-150 version.
2. Long-wheelbase Club Wagons could seat from five to 12 passengers. Econoline engines included a 300-cubic-inch six and 351- and 460-cid V-8s.

1975

1. The F-Series pickup line changed little for 1975, with one exception: added was an F-150 model, which was intended to split the difference in payload capacity between the F-100 and F-250. Though hardly a major event at the time, the F-150 would eventually take over from the F-100 as Ford's base full-size pickup, and go on to become the best-selling vehicle in the United States. 2-3. Bronco likewise received few changes for 1975, though front disc brakes were made available late in the model year.

1976

1976: F-Series pickup offerings expand with the addition of four-wheel-drive F-150 models and the return of a short-bed Flareside F-100; fans of the current custom-van craze are courted with the Cruising Van; Courier compact pickup gets larger cab and revised appearance details

The first styling facelift to the 1973-generation F-Series light-duty trucks showed up for '76, when a new grille and squarish headlamp bezels appeared. F-100s with four-wheel drive, like this long-bed Ranger XLT, came with a standard 360-cubic-inch V-8 and four-speed transmission.

1976

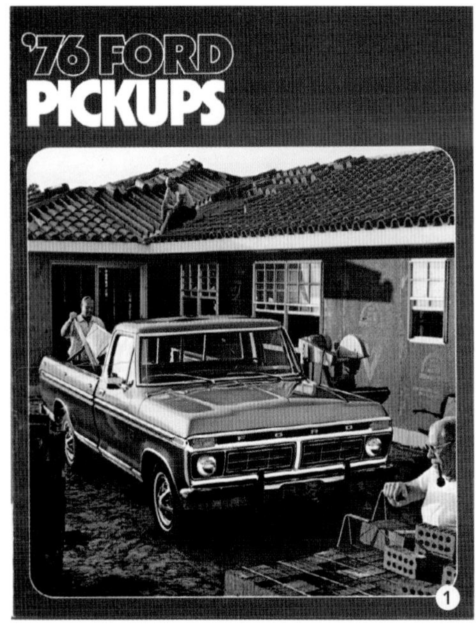

1. The expanded line of F-Series pickups was covered in this 16-page catalog. 2. Four-wheel-drive F-150s were initially offered only in long-bed form (shown), though a short-bed version was added midyear. 3. The Mazda-built Courier got a revised grille and a three-inch-longer cab that allowed for more seat travel. 4. An F-100 regular cab is shown with the optional tool-storage box and Deluxe Tu-Tone paint. 5. The short-wheelbase F-100 Flareside returned after a three-year hiatus. A pin-stripe option package was added midyear.

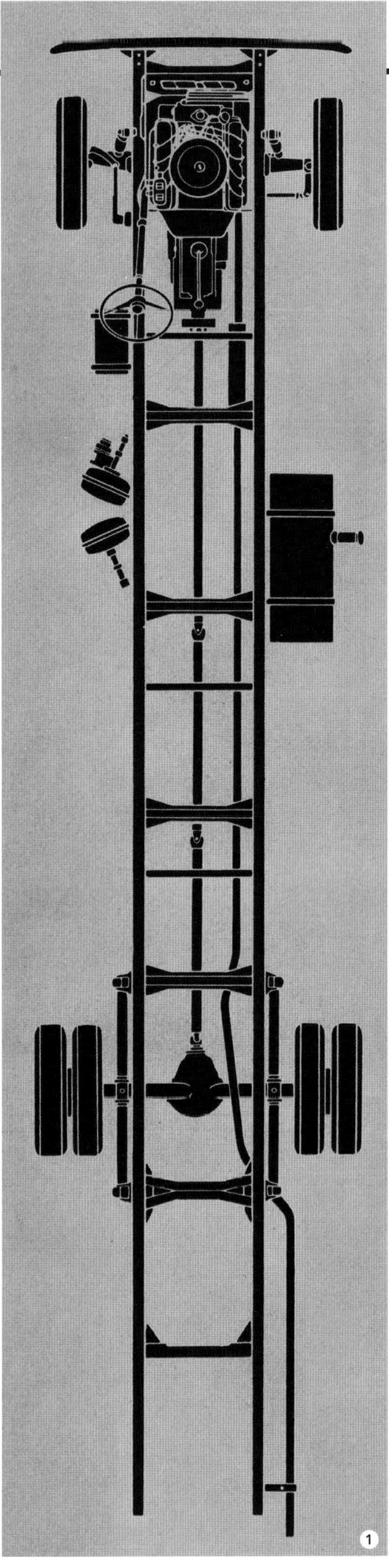

1-2. Shown is a sketch of the B-Series school bus chassis as it appeared in the commercial-chassis brochure for '76. The bus platform was available in a choice of six wheelbase lengths. 3. The Bronco, now 10 years old, featured optional front disc brakes. 4. The L-Line grew with the addition of the LTL-9000. This new linehauler, distinguished by its lengthened nose, came with a Cummins NTC-350 diesel engine and 10-speed Fuller Roadranger transmission as standard equipment.

1977

1977: Ford creates expressive "Free Wheeling" decor packages for pickups, vans, and Pinto wagons; stripped Econoline E-250 and E-350 chassis replace long-serving P-Series parcel deliveries; consolidation of models sweeps through medium- and heavy-duty ranks; Courier adds long-bed version

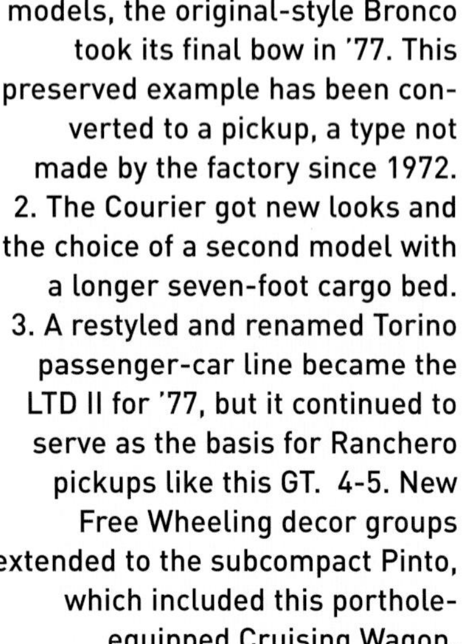

1. With the sport-utility-vehicle market shifting toward larger models, the original-style Bronco took its final bow in '77. This preserved example has been converted to a pickup, a type not made by the factory since 1972. 2. The Courier got new looks and the choice of a second model with a longer seven-foot cargo bed. 3. A restyled and renamed Torino passenger-car line became the LTD II for '77, but it continued to serve as the basis for Ranchero pickups like this GT. 4-5. New Free Wheeling decor groups extended to the subcompact Pinto, which included this porthole-equipped Cruising Wagon.

1-2. Though touched on only lightly in the 1977 F-Series pickup catalog, four-wheel-drive models (including the Bronco) were attracting enough interest to warrant a brochure of their own. 3. An F-100 "Shorty Flareside" with four-wheel drive shows off the flashy graphics and abundant accessory choices that were aimed at younger buyers who wanted to personalize their trucks. The 117-inch-wheelbase Flareside featured a 6½-foot cargo bed. 4-5. A "low-profile" four-wheel-drive F-250 with reduced ride height was introduced in April '77.

1. Econolines became popular for aftermarket van conversions. Three available trailering packages let them tow as much as 10,000 lbs. 2-3. The F-600, which was available with a crew cab, took over at the bottom of the revised medium-duty F-Series when the F-500 was dropped. 4, 7. The W-Series was offered with a number of Owner-Operator paint schemes. 5. C-Series Tilt Cabs were sold with Caterpillar diesel engines in three horsepower ratings or six gasoline V-8s. 6. Ford linehaulers began with the bigger of the L-Line models.

Ford F-Series

3

1977

4

5

6

7

1978

1978: A larger, heavier, and more powerful Bronco replaces Ford's original compact sport-utility vehicle; F-Series light-duty models adopt new grille design and some shift to rectangular headlamps; Econoline Super Wagon and Super Van with rear-body extension debut; CL- and CLT-9000 replace W-Series linehaulers as Ford's biggest trucks

1. The Courier compact pickup had a new grille design that incorporated the parking lamps. The XLT version flashed lots of bright trim on the outside and woodgrain accents on the inside. 2. Free Wheeling packages spiced up the Courier with stripes and special trim. 3. Color and optional equipment shuffles were about all that was new for the Ranchero. 4. Ford's car/pickup was turned into this mean-looking Viper show vehicle. 5-7. A new 104-inch-wheelbase Bronco was derived from F-Series trucks. A 351-cubic-inch V-8 was standard, with a 400 cid available.

5

6

7

1978

1

2

3

4

5

1-2. The plush Ranger Lariat was the new top level of the F-Series light-duty line. 3. A new grille shape with a hint of the L-Line trucks was applied to light-duty F models. All but base Customs used rectangular headlamps.
4. White, black, or gold pinstriping was available on Free Wheeling Flaresides. 5. The '78 version of the Explorer dress-up package is shown on an F-150 Ranger.
6. Free Wheeling Styleside pickups bore bold rainbow stripes.
7. Big Louisville rigs inspired the F-250 Little Louie show truck.
8. Econoline vans could be fitted with rear "porthole" windows and special trim. 9. Super Wagons featured 20 extra inches of rear body.

1978

1

2

3

4

1. F-350 Stake Bed and Platform models were newly equipped with a frame-mounted fuel tank. 2. A new truck advertising slogan—"Built Ford Tough"—certainly applied to medium-duties like this F-600 crew cab. 3. Even the utilitarian C-Series could be dressed up with a Custom Cab option and other brightwork. 4, 6. L-Line trucks were offered with increased Gross Vehicle Weight Ratings for 1978. 5. The CLT-9000 became Ford's top linehauler. The aerodynamic aluminum CL cab could be ordered with air springs to smooth out road shocks.

5

6

1979: Ranchero's 22-year run as Ford's car-based pickup comes to an end; four-wheel-drive availability extended to F-350 one-ton pickups; Econolines get new eggcrate grille and rectangular headlamps; second-row captain's-chair option made available for Econoline vans and Club Wagons; new line of gasoline V-8s introduced for C, F, and L models

1979

1. A 2.0-liter overhead-camshaft four was installed as the new base engine in the Courier. 2. The grille style and graphics of the Pinto Cruising Wagon were revised for '79. 3-4. When the LTD II car line ceased production at the end of 1979, it took the Ranchero pickup with it. A GT model was offered to the end. 5. The Captain's Club Wagon featured two-tone paint, tinted rear-body glass, and four swiveling high-backed captain's chairs. 6-7. E-Series vans and wagons of various sizes served the needs of the fun-loving and the family oriented.

1979
5

FORD
Firestone
1979
6

FORD
1979
7

1979

FORD
F-SERIES

5

8

6

1. An F-150 Ranger Lariat could get optional Combination Tu-Tone paint and bright box rails. 2. As four-wheel drive gained acceptance, Ford added it to F-350 pickups. 3. A two-wheel-drive F-150 Ranger XLT Super Cab shows its length. 4. Rectangular headlights were extended to F-Series Customs for '79. This F-100 Flareside shows the Free Wheeling stripe pattern. 5-7. Ford offered medium-duty conventionals in both the F-Series and L-Line. The CL-9000 Cab-Over-Engine (COE) was considered a heavy-duty model. 8-9. Bronco Ranger XLTs with, respectively, Combination Tu-Tone and Free Wheeling decor.

7

9

Chapter Eight: 1980-1989

Satisfying the Market with Downsizing and Design

Ford's primary focus during the 1980s was on fuel economy, a fact substantiated by styling changes, revised powertrains, and the development of smaller offerings.

Greeting the new decade was a restyled F-Series pickup with a more aerodynamic front end. Cabs were a bit bigger, too, and four-wheel-drive versions got independent front suspension in the form of Ford's Twin Traction Beam setup. Late in the 1980 model year, medium- and heavy-duty trucks were offered with engines that ran on Liquid Propane (LP) Gas.

Added as an F-100 option for 1981 was a "downsized" 255-cubic-inch V-8. Smaller than even the standard 300-cubic-inch six, it may have been more marketing hype than fuel-economy help, but it showed Ford's commitment to increasing gas mileage.

1980-1989

Chapter Eight

Even more of a commitment was shown for 1983 when the slow-selling Mazda-built Courier was replaced by the Ford-built Ranger, which quickly became the most popular compact pickup in the land. Further testament appeared the following year when the Ranger-based Bronco II sport-utility vehicle was added to the lineup. Both the Ranger and Bronco II carried styling cues that linked them to their F-Series and Bronco big brothers, which was probably both helpful and intentional.

Another bit of noteworthy news for 1984 came not in the form of a change or addition, but of a loss. The Ford F-100, a model name that had been around since 1953, was discontinued, probably because its gross vehicle Weight fell below the threshold that would have allowed it to get by on the less-stringent emission standards that applied to heavier-duty trucks. But this was more of a historical loss than a sales one, as the slightly beefier F-150, which had been introduced in 1975, absorbed those buyers—as evidenced by the fact it would soon become the nation's best-selling full-size pickup, and soon after the best-selling vehicle of any type.

Fuel injection arrived for 1985, but only on selected engines: the 5.0-liter (302-cubic-inch) V-8 in F-Series and Bronco, and the 2.3-liter four in the Ranger. More engines adopted it over the next few years, and all were fuel injected by the end of the decade.

In response to the surprisingly popular Dodge Caravan and Plymouth Voyager minivans introduced by Chrysler Corporation in 1984, Ford brought out the Aerostar for 1986. Being built on a rear-wheel-drive truck frame, the Aerostar was closer to a traditional van than the front-drive/unibody Chryslers, and that—along with its available V-6—gave it a higher towing capacity.

The year also brought a new name to Ford's medium-duty truck lineup: the Cargo. Unusual in that it carried a name rather than a series designation, it was referred to as a "low tilt cab," though the cab was in fact rather tall. Designed around European styling themes, the

Cargo was intended to replace the boxy ´50s-vintage C-Series Tilt Cab—still in production—but the two were sold side-by-side through the end of the decade. Also new that year was a SuperCab version of the Ranger pickup.

Ford's 1987 light-duty F-Series trucks and their full-size Bronco companions were treated to a long-awaited restyle, again getting more-aerodynamic front ends. They also got rear-wheel antilock brakes, as did the Bronco II. Also in 1987, Henry Ford II, who had taken over and essentially "saved" Ford Motor Company in the 1940s and ran it until 1980, died of pneumonia at the age of 70.

A new line of Super Duty F-350 trucks was introduced for the 1988 model year. These trucks filled a gap between the regular F-350s and the medium-duty F-600s. Standard was a 7.5-liter V-8, while a 7.3-liter diesel was optional. F-Series also dropped its available Flareside bed, though it would return a few years later.

Bigger news for 1988—literally— was the introduction of a sleek new Class 8 truck called the AeroMax. Though the cab was similar to that used for its L-Series Louisville stablemates, the front end was given an aero look and the interior was spruced up.

For 1989, the Bronco II and Ranger were restyled for the first time since their introduction, getting—you guessed it—aerodynamically sleeker front ends. Ranger also added the standard rear-wheel antilock brakes the Bronco II had received two years earlier. New for the Aerostar minivan was a "midi" version with a longer body.

As the decade wound to a close, Ford found itself in a rather enviable position. The F-Series was established as the nation's best-selling vehicle, the Ranger was the best-selling compact pickup, and the rest of the trucks—all the way up to the heavy-duty Class 8 entries—were strong competitors in their respective segments. All in all, Ford was in fine fettle to enter the Nineties.

1980

1980: Styling revised on F-Series/Bronco, and 4×4 versions get independent front suspension

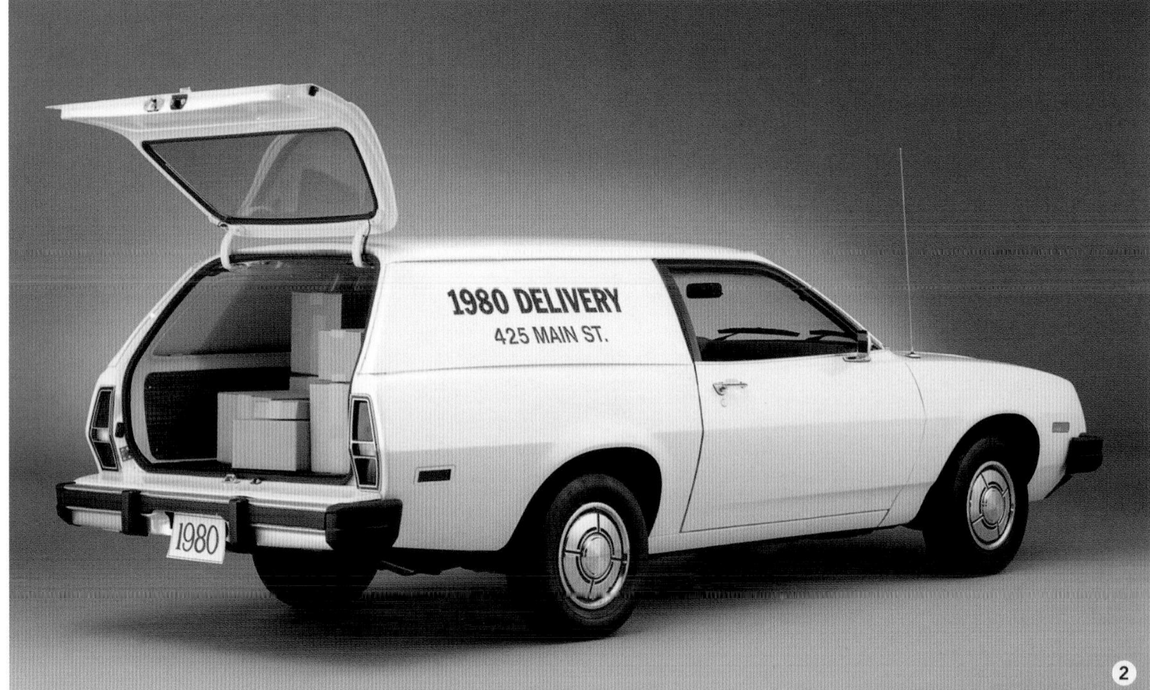

1. Coors Beer commissioned a custom Courier that featured period-popular hood scoop, spoilers, sunroof, and big-rig-style chrome exhaust stacks. The Flareside bed was specially made, as it wasn't offered on Courier that year. 2. With fuel economy a high priority in the early Eighties, a thrifty Pinto Delivery was a wise choice for hauling small items. 3. Put a porthole in a Delivery, add stripes and fancy wheels, and it becomes a Cruising Wagon. By combining elements of the van craze with four-cylinder economy, Ford's stylish cruiser—which was introduced in the mid Seventies—carried through to 1980, Pinto's swan-song year. The 2.8-liter V-6 option was dropped, leaving a 2.3-liter four as the only engine choice. 4. A van was just a van, but the addition of portholes, tape stripes, and fancy wheels meant you were "Vanning"—which was something else entirely. Interiors usually received even more attention than exteriors. 5-8. Broncos and F-Series pickups got a new face for 1980. Pickups continued to offer both Styleside and Flareside beds.

4

5

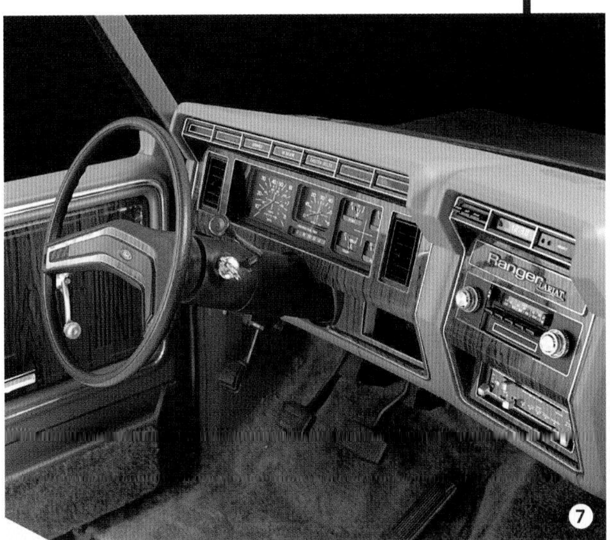

7

6

8

1980

1. Bronco and F-Series four-wheel-drive models adopted Twin-Traction Beam independent front suspension for 1980. Rival GM 4×4s wouldn't get independent front suspension until 1988. 2. Ford redesigned its medium-duty trucks for 1980, giving them a sleek, modern look that bore a kinship to their heavy-duty siblings. Both gas and diesel engines were offered.

1981

1981: All truck lines carry over virtually unchanged, though F-100 adds an economy-minded 255-cubic-inch V-8

F-Series trucks had long received an annual styling update—even if it only amounted to a slight change in the grille—but that practice ceased with the 1981 models, which were virtually identical to the 1980's. By this time, the F-Series was on a roll as the best-selling truck in the land, so there was little incentive to mess with success. Besides, the 1980-81 was a good-looking design, as evidenced by this two-tone F-150 Flareside.

1981

1. With fuel economy a hot topic, Ford added a small, 255-cubic-inch V-8 as a 1981 option for F-100s. The standard engine remained a 300-cid six in most light-duty pickups, with 302- and 351-cid V-8s optional. F-350s could also be ordered with a 400-cid V-8. 2-4. Several custom decor packages were available for light-duty pickups that included two-tone paint, tape stripes, blackout grille, and white-painted or aluminum wheels. Flareside beds, once considered more utilitarian than the smooth-sided Styleside versions, were now considered more stylish. 5. As for its F-150 counterpart, the 1981 Bronco looked the same as the 1980 version.

4

5

1981

1. Introduced for 1976, the LTL-9000 remained Ford's top-line heavy-duty truck in the early Eighties. It came standard with many custom touches—both inside and out—and was marked by squared-off grille and fenders that capped an extended-length front end. 2. Econoline styling was unaltered for 1981, as was most of the rest of the van, and it remained the best-selling full-size van in the United States. A 300-cubic-inch six was standard, but most Econolines had the 302- or 351-cid V-8, while E-350s could get up to a 460-cid V-8.

1982

1982: Final year for Courier pickup; mildly restyled front end for F-Series and Bronco

1. An ´82 F-series differed in appearance from an ´81 courtesy of a Ford blue oval that was placed in the center of a grille with fewer vertical bars. This prompted the deletion of the Ford lettering that previously graced the leading edge of the hood. In a further bow to fuel economy, the F-100 came standard with a new 232-cubic-inch V-6 for 1982. 2. SuperCabs had a longer cab that allowed for a three-passenger rear bench seat or a pair of jump seats. The divided rear side window first appeared for 1980.

1982

1. Spoked wheels and tape stripes continued to dress up F-Series trucks, with some new designs being offered for 1982. During this time, pickups were becoming more popular for regular passenger use, largely replacing high-performance cars—long since regulated out of existence—as trendy transportation. 2. Econoline vans didn't change much for 1982, not even getting the new grille treatment that graced their F-Series siblings. 3. As usual, Bronco carried the front-end look of the F-Series. Engine choices remained a 300-cubic-inch six, or V-8s of 302 and 351 cid. 4. Medium-duty F-Series trucks shared the cab but not the front end of the F-Series pickups, getting instead a taller grille and wider fenders. F-600, -700, and -800 models spanned a GVW range of 24,500 to 31,000 lbs, and the 700 was offered in a 4×4 version. Gasoline, LP, diesel, and turbodiesel engines were available.

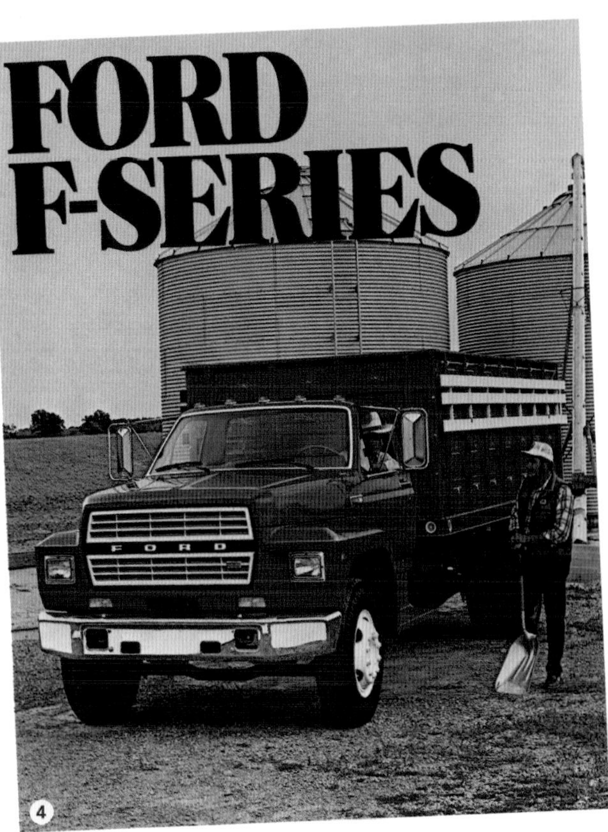

1-2. Covering a similar 24,000- to 27,500-lb GVW range were the big-rig-styled LN-Series medium-duty trucks. From the front bumper to the back of the cab, they were about seven inches shorter than their F-Series counterparts. 3. Ford's own 8.2-liter (500-cubic-inch) diesel was offered in F- and LN-Series trucks in either normally aspirated (165 horsepower) or turbocharged (205 hp) form. Gas engines were also available. 4. Offered in the LN-Series was a Caterpillar 3208 V-8 diesel with 165 to 200 horsepower. The Cat provided a broad torque range that minimized shifting in city traffic. 5. The biggest dog on Ford's block was the LTL-9000, which could be dressed up with a number of paint and striping themes. LTLs were exclusively diesel powered, with engines by Cummins (300 to 400 horsepower), Caterpillar (350 to 400 hp), and Detroit Diesel (365 to 445 hp).

3

4

2

5

1983

1983: Ranger compact pickup replaces Courier; higher GVW F-Series medium-duty trucks introduced

1. In an effort to reduce drag, a pickup undergoes wind tunnel testing. With many customers showing increased interest in fuel economy, even trucks were tweaked for maximum efficiency. 2-3. Replacing the Mazda-built Courier for 1983 was the Ford-built Ranger. Introduced early in the 1982 calendar year, the Ranger was nearly the same size as the Courier and also offered six- and seven-foot beds. Unlike the Courier, however, it was available not only with regular four-cylinder engines, but also with a V-6 or four-cylinder diesel engine, and—later in the model year—with four-wheel drive.

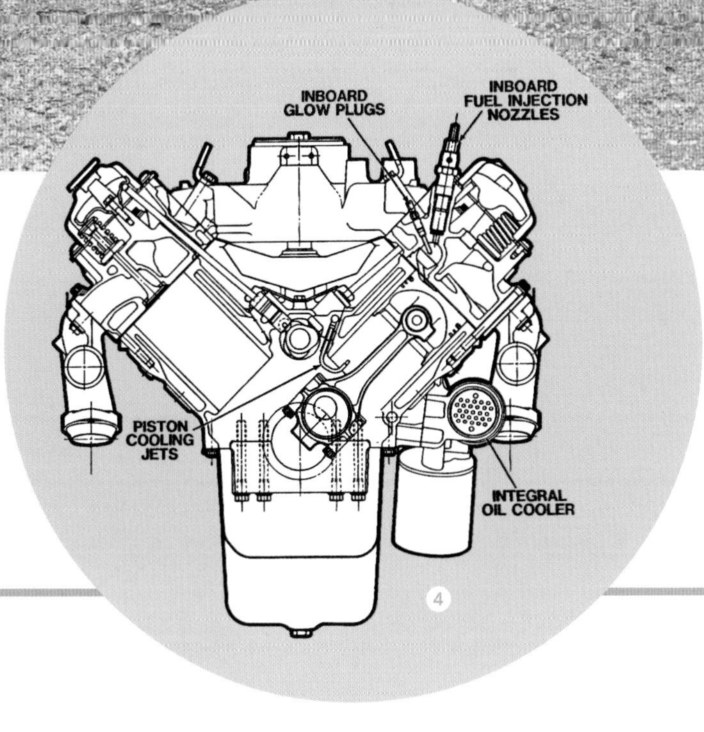

1. For 1983, Econolines finally adopted the Ford grille badge fitted to F-Series pickups the previous year. 2. Aside from some trim variations, Bronco stood pat for 1983. 3. Among F-Series pickups, only the F-350 was available in a four-door, six-passenger crew-cab body style for 1983. All 350s also came with an eight-foot bed, meaning the truck pictured stretched more than 237 inches—just shy of 20 feet—bumper-to-bumper. 4. Optional on the F-250 Heavy Duty and F-350 was Ford's 6.9-liter diesel V-8.

1983

New for the 1983 F-Series medium-duty line was a trio of trucks with GVW ratings that edged them into the heavy-duty range. The FT-800 and FT-900 were tandem-axle vehicles with gasoline engines; the FT-8000 (pictured) was a tandem with diesel engine.

1984

1984: Bronco II compact SUV debuts; venerable F-100 pickup dropped, as is E-100 van

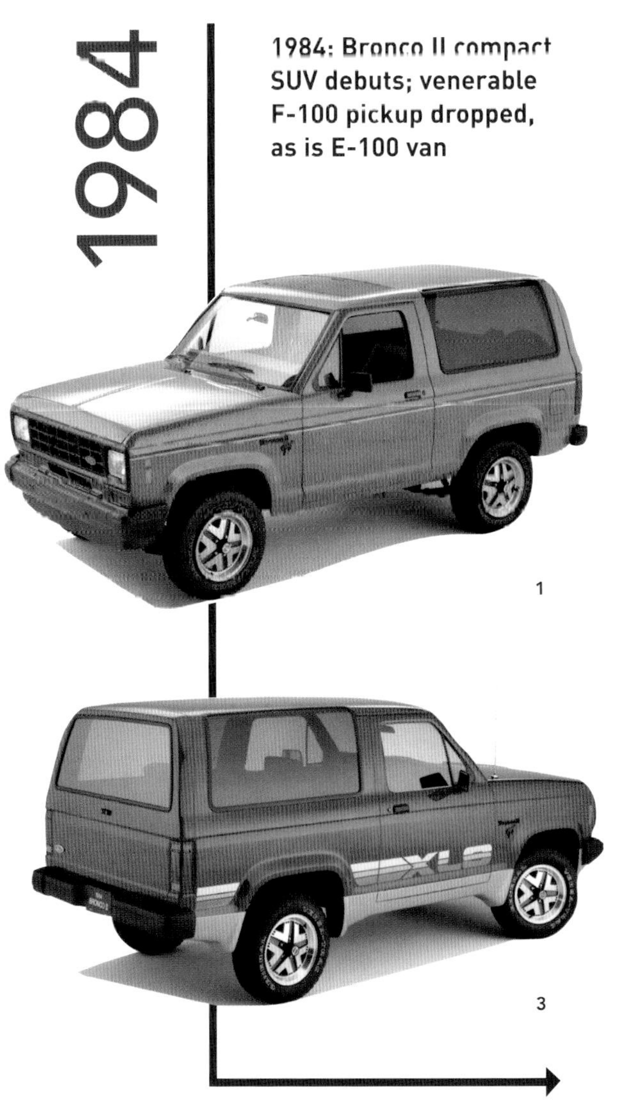

1

3

2

4

5

1-3. Ford entered the compact-SUV arena with the 1984 Bronco II. Introduced early in the 1983 calendar year, it closely followed the Chevrolet S-10 Blazer/GMC Jimmy to market in what was essentially a new segment—and was closely followed by the Jeep Cherokee. All were designed in response to the 1979 gas crisis, which is why these direct competitors went on sale at about the same time. Bronco II was based on the compact Ranger pickup, introduced the previous year. All models came with four-wheel drive and a 2.8-liter (171-cubic inch) V-6. Compared to its big Bronco brother, the Bronco II was shorter by 10 inches in wheelbase and 19 inches in overall length, and—most significantly—lighter by more than 800 lbs. A sporty XLS package added tri-color tape stripes and wheelwell "spats."

4-5. After siring its SUV stablemate, Ranger was given a rest for 1984, seeing no significant changes. Note the similarities between the Ranger and Bronco II, particularly from the cab forward.

1984

1. The most significant change to the Econoline for 1984 was the deletion of the base E-100 model; the line now started with the E-150. Econolines were offered in two wheelbases and three overall lengths. Shown is an E-250 Super window van. Though they rode the same longer wheelbase as "regulars," Supers carried a 20-inch-longer body. In the case of passenger models, this extra length allowed for an additional bench seat in back, boosting capacity from 12 people to 15. 2. The full-size Bronco remained in a rut, as it once again didn't see any significant changes—and hadn't since 1980. It retained its removable rear roof section, which allowed the back seat and cargo area to be uncovered. 3-4. Because the F-100's GVW rating put it below the threshold that allowed heavier pickups to get by with meeting "looser" truck emission standards, the model was unceremoniously dropped for 1984—after 30 years on the market. With that, the F-150 became Ford's base full-size pickup. Options included Explorer special-value packages that provided numerous uplevel features at a discounted price.

3

4

Donald E. Petersen
President

Ford Motor Company
The American Road
Dearborn, Michigan 48121

Dear New Truck Buyer:

Quality is Job 1 at Ford Motor Company. This isn't just a phrase. It's a commitment to total quality.

Total quality begins with the design and engineering of our trucks and continues through the life of the product. We plan them with a vision of the customer—of you—sitting behind the wheel of a new truck.

Total quality will be apparent to you through functional performance, overall vehicle integrity, the "look and feel" of materials, satisfying aesthetics, safety, serviceability and cost of ownership.

Total quality requires continuous improvement in everything we do. Every employee at Ford Motor Company is involved in the process of meeting your needs and expectations.

I invite you to look over our new 1985 Ford trucks in your dealer's showroom. Test drive them on the road. When you do, I think you'll understand all that's involved in the total quality concept at Ford Motor Company.

Donald E. Petersen
President
Ford Motor Company

1

1985

1985: Fuel-injected truck engines debut

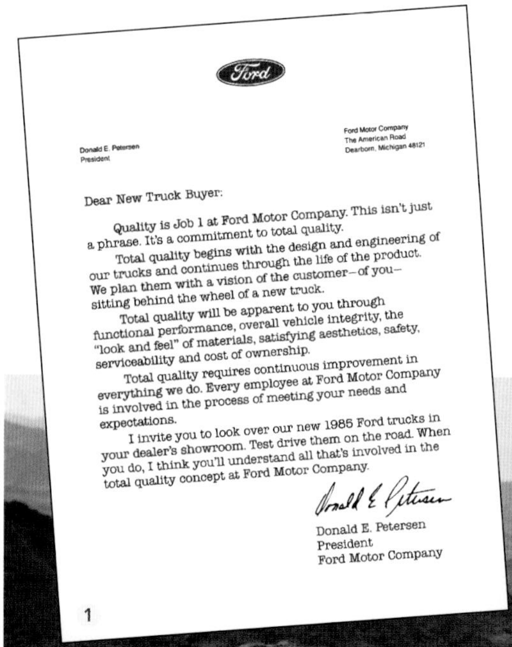

2

1. Donald E. Peterson, president of Ford Motor Company, released this letter that included Ford's famous "Quality is Job 1" slogan. 2. F-Series pickups offered an optional fuel-injected 5.0-liter engine for 1985 and F-350 crew cabs got a dual-rear-wheel option, but otherwise the line saw few changes. Other gas engines remained carbureted. 3. Newly standard for the 1985 Ranger was a fuel-injected 2.3-liter four-cylinder that was more powerful than the carbureted version it replaced. A carbureted 2.8-liter V-6 remained optional. Newly available was a four-speed automatic transmission.

3

1. Aside from a five-speed manual transmission replacing a four-speed as standard, and the newly available four-speed automatic as an option, Bronco II saw few changes for 1985. It could look quite ritzy when dressed up with optional decor packages. 2. Big-brother Bronco got some new dress-up packages along with the optional fuel-injected 5.0-liter V-8 offered in the F-Series pickups. 3. Econoline stood pat for 1985, not even getting the fuel-injected V-8 available in its full-size Bronco/F-Series siblings. 4. Now looking like something out of a trucking time warp, the tried-and-true C-Series Tilt Cab, which dated from 1957, continued in Ford's lineup—mostly because it continued to be popular.

1986

1986: Aerostar minivan debuts; Ranger adds SuperCab versions, a fuel injected V-6, and shift-on-the-fly four-wheel drive; Bronco II adds the same V-6 and 4×4 system; medium-duty Cargo line introduced

1. Ford brought out the 1986 Aerostar to compete with the highly successful Dodge Caravan/Plymouth Voyager minivans. But while its Chrysler Corporation counterparts were front-wheel drive, the Aerostar was rear-wheel drive. Like its rivals, Aerostar came with a sliding right-side door. Standard was a 2.3-liter four, with a 2.8-liter V-6 optional. 2. Aerostar was also available in a cargo version with blanked-out side windows. 3. With the F-150 firmly ensconced as the best-selling vehicle in the U.S., there was little reason to change it for 1986—and Ford didn't.

1. Ranger offered a SuperCab body style for 1986 that added 17 inches to the back of the cab. A pair of rear jump seats was optional. SuperCabs came only with a six-foot bed; regular cabs also offered a seven-footer. Newly available on the base Ranger S was a 2.0-liter four, while other models came with a 2.3-liter four or new fuel-injected 2.9-liter V-6. Also offered that year—but rarely ordered—was a 2.3-liter turbodiesel. Four-wheel-drive Rangers got a new "shift-on-the-fly" system. The V-6 and diesel engines, along with the 4×4 system, were shared with the Ranger's Bronco II stablemate. 2. Newly offered on Ford's heavy-duty Cab-Over-Engine models for 1986 were aftercooler systems that coaxed more power and better fuel economy out of their diesel engines. Available options now included a chrome front bumper and exterior-mounted sun visor (both fitted to the CLT-9000 shown), along with a Jacobs Engine Brake. A "Jake Brake," as it was often called, used the engine's compression to help slow the vehicle when coming to a stop.

1987

1987: F-Series and Bronco treated to first major styling changes since 1980, along with standard fuel injection and rear-wheel antilock brakes; Aerostar gets fuel-injected V-6; Bronco II adds two-wheel-drive version and rear-wheel antilock brakes

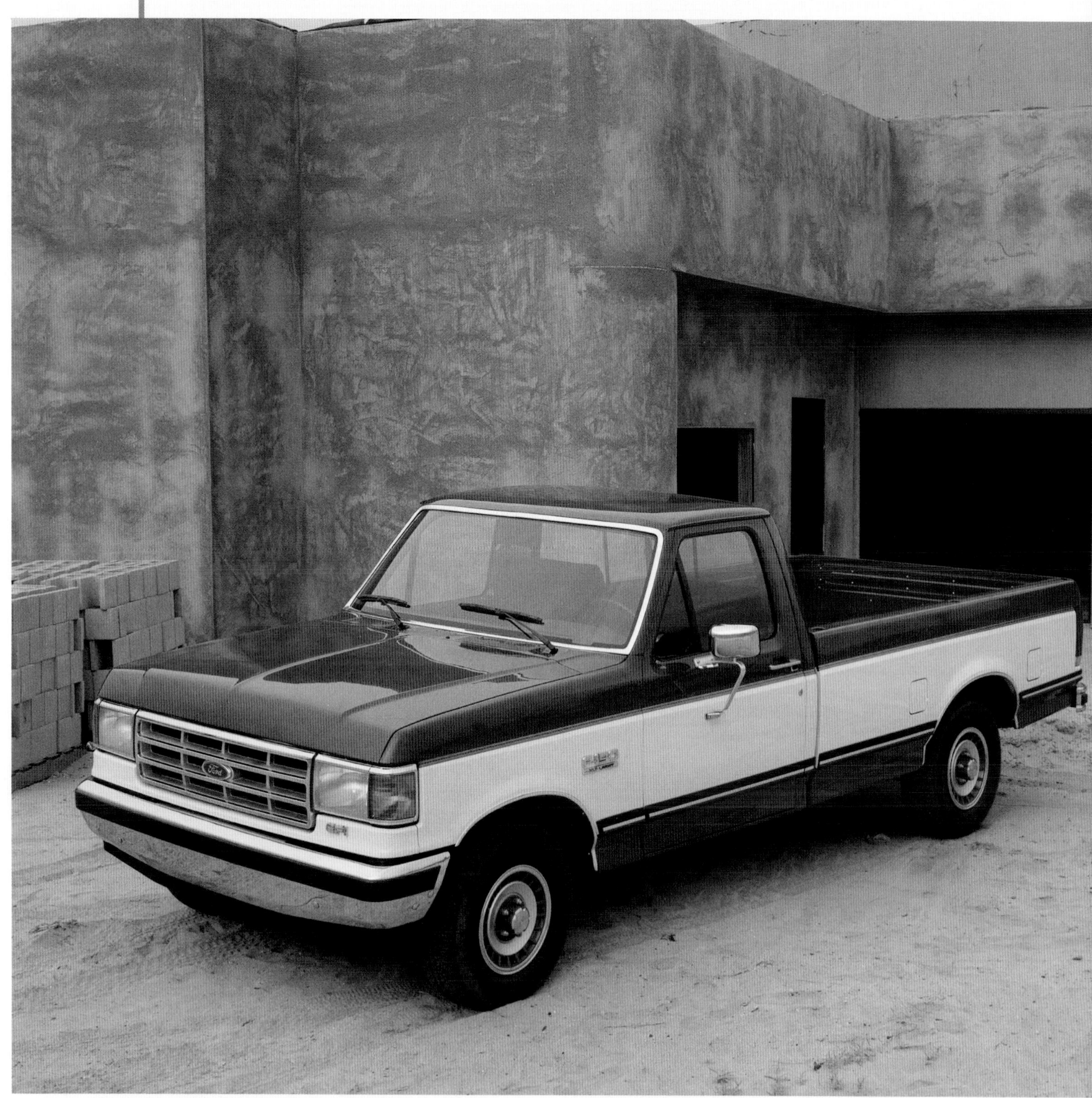

1-2. In their first major update since 1980, Ford's F-Series trucks got an aerodynamic restyle for 1987 that featured rounded-off front corners and flush-mounted headlights. Interiors were also redesigned. The base 4.9-liter six gained fuel injection—and a 25 percent increase in horsepower—and rear-wheel antilock brakes were added as standard equipment. 3. SuperCabs continued with their divided rear side windows. An available rear bench could seat up to three passengers. 4. Those same three passengers would have a lot more room in an F-350 crew cab. Optional was a 6.9-liter diesel V-8 built by International Harvester. Dual rear wheels for this model were made available beginning in 1985.

2

3

4

1987

1. Bronco got the same front-end and interior restyle as the F-Series pickups, along with standard rear-wheel antilock brakes and fuel-injected six-cylinder engine.
2. Originally planned for 1986, but not arriving until ´87, was a two-wheel-drive version of the Bronco II. Also new for ´87 were the addition of rear-wheel antilock brakes and availability of an electronically shifted four-wheel-drive transfer case.

1. Ranger offered an off-road-flavored High Rider package that included a bed-mounted light bar and tubular grille guard. 2. Econoline's standard 4.9-liter six gained fuel injection for '87, but little else changed. Load space inside this E-250 Super Cargo Van was cavernous. 3. A fuel-injected 3.0-liter V-6 became standard on passenger versions of the Aerostar for 1987. It was optional on cargo versions, which came with a 2.3-liter four. Newly optional were special rear seats that converted into a bed.

1987

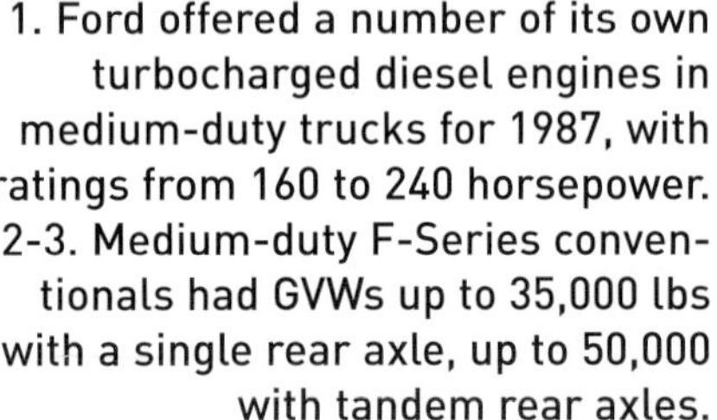

1. Ford offered a number of its own turbocharged diesel engines in medium-duty trucks for 1987, with ratings from 160 to 240 horsepower.
2-3. Medium-duty F-Series conventionals had GVWs up to 35,000 lbs with a single rear axle, up to 50,000 with tandem rear axles.

1. The B-Series bus chassis carried an F-Series front end, but everything from the windshield back was supplied by an aftermarket manufacturer. 2-3. Joining the aging C-Series Tilt Cab forward-control truck for 1986 was the similar, but more modern looking Cargo; shown is a 1987 model. Though probably intended to replace the C-Series, the two were sold side-by-side through the end of the decade. 4. Representing Ford's medium-duty lineup are (left to right) an L-8000 with set-back front axle, Cargo, and F-Series.

1987

1

1. Ford's medium-duty L-Series trucks showed a variety of faces for 1987. Some received styling updates that year, which included a horizontal-bar grille and, on models without a setback front axle (such as shown here), rectangular headlights. 2. Other '87 L-Series models retained the previous- year's look. 3. Class-8 trucks are the biggest available, and Ford offered both Cab-Over-Engine (COE) and conventional models in that segment. The COE was the CLT-9000; shown is a Ford-owned rig on a promotional tour of the United States.
4-5. Ford's Class-8 conventional was the LTL-9000. For 1987, it offered a revised cabin and dashboard (6), while a dash with added instrumentation (7) was optional. Also new that year were improved Cummins and Caterpillar diesel engines with up to 400 horsepower.

2

1988

1988: Flareside bed dropped; heavier-duty F-350s released; "light-heavy-duty" L-7000 introduced; heavy-duty AeroMax debuts

1. Ford dropped its stylish Flareside bed for 1988, meaning all pickups carried the Styleside bed shown on the F-150 pictured. All engines now boasted fuel injection, but otherwise, the F-Series was little-changed after its 1987 facelift.
2. F-350s were offered with GVW ratings of up to 14,500 lbs. for 1988, made possible with the addition of available four-wheel disc brakes, heavy-duty axles, and 16-inch wheels. The optional diesel V-8 grew from 6.9 liters to 7.3.

1. Ranger was a virtual carryover for 1988, though newly available for two-wheel-drive regular cabs was a GT package with sport suspension, front spoiler, and side skirts. 2. Aside from some minor trim details, the Bronco II was likewise a rerun. 3. Like the F-Series, the Bronco carried into 1988 with few changes except that all engines were now fuel injected.

1

2

1988

1. Topping the L-Series line for '88 was the L-9000; the version shown is equipped with a setback front axle, which allowed for a tighter turning radius. 2. The L-7000 was a lighter-duty version of the heavy-duty L-Series line that effectively fell into the medium-duty segment. Confusing, perhaps, but it made sense to a lot of buyers. 3. New to the Cargo line of medium-duty trucks for 1988 were a couple of heavier-duty models called the CF-8000 (single rear axle) and CFT-8000 (tandem rear axles). They replaced the C-800 version of the '50s-vintage Tilt Cab.

3

1. Slipping into the limelight for 1988 was the AeroMax, which upped the ante in Class-8 aerodynamics. Featuring swept-back front fenders and a form-fitting front bumper—both made possible by the setback front axle—it made for a sleek update to what was essentially an L-Series truck. Wraparound headlights added a modern look, while tank skirts and an available "Aero Bullet" sleeper unit made the AeroMax more slippery to the wind. 2. The LTL-9000 long-nose conventional remained Ford's top Class-8 truck in many driver's eyes, despite its new AeroMax challenger.

1988

1989

1989: Ranger and Bronco II restyled; Ranger gets standard antilock rear brakes; Aerostar adds extended version

1. After many stand-pat years on the styling front, Ranger finally got a sleek new front end for 1989 that mimicked the look of its F-Series big brother. Interiors were also new, as were the standard antilock rear brakes. A twin-plug head on the 2.3-liter four boosted horsepower by 10 to an even 100. A 140-hp 2.9-liter V-6 was also available.
2. Bronco II shared Ranger's restyled front end and interior, but little else was new.

1989

1. Aerostars boasted a new front-end look for 1989, courtesy of a restyled grille and a slot integrated into the front bumper. It was hardly a dramatic change. 2. Somewhat more noticeable was the new extended-length version of the Aerostar, which added 15 inches behind the rear axle for increased cargo space. It also allowed for a slight increase in second- and third-row leg room. 3. Passenger versions of the Econoline were called Club Wagons. On E-250 and E-350 versions, a four-speed automatic transmission was newly available when the big 7.5-liter V-8 was ordered. 4. Cargo models were called Econoline Vans, and that same powertrain combination was offered on E-350 models.

1-2. Two-wheel-drive versions of the F-150 wore "EFI" (Electronic Fuel Injection) badges below the left-side headlight (1), while four-wheel drives had a "4×4" badge (2). Expanded availability of the four-speed automatic transmission to heavy-duty two-wheel-drive models was the only change of note to F-Series pickups for 1989. 3. Bronco carried over virtually unchanged for 1989. It offered a number of powertrain choices, including a 4.9-liter six, 5.0 V-8, and 5.8 V-8 (all fuel injected), along with four- and five-speed manual transmissions and three- or four-speed automatics.

Chapter Nine: 1990-1999

Introductions and Fond Farewells

It wasn't long after the Nineties began that Ford introduced what would become one of the most significant vehicles in its long history. But as it so happened, that debut coincided with the loss of a couple of long-time favorites.

Toward the end of the 1990 model year, Ford released a new sport-utility vehicle called the Explorer. Available in both two- and four-door form, it was labeled a 1991 model and would quickly become the best-selling SUV in the U.S., a title it has garnered every year since. But it spelled the end of the smaller two-door Bronco II, which had amassed its own devote following with its tidy size and reasonable fuel efficiency. And shortly thereafter, Ford announced that the beloved medium-duty C-Series Tilt Cab, which was introduced for 1957 and had soldiered on for more than 30 years with hardly a change or complaint, was to be decommissioned.

Ford celebrated its 75th anniversary of being in the truck business during 1992, a year that also brought a redesign of the full-size Econoline vans. These vehicles had not seen major changes since 1975, so it was a welcome modernization.

The 1993 model year brought a similar update for the Ranger compact pickup, which had seen few changes since its 1983 introduction. It also brought the debut of a high-performance F-150—an oxymoron to some—called the Lightning. Ford's Special Vehicle Team built it for buyers who wanted the utility of a truck with the power and handling of a performance car. The Lightning would come and go over the years, but it would always stay true to its originally stated mission.

1990-1999

Chapter Nine

Safety was highlighted for 1994, as the Econoline gained four-wheel antilock brakes and the F-Series pickups got a driver-side airbag.

Ford added a more modern minivan to its line for 1995. Called the Windstar, this front-wheel-drive people-mover was initially intended to replace the aging Aerostar, but the latter's continued popularity made it the Windstar's running mate until finally being retired after 1997.

Though the Explorer was still the number-one seller in its market segment, Ford elected to freshen its appearance for the 1995 model year. Also newly available that year was a flexible-fuel version (FFV) that could run on a mixture of gasoline and ethanol, the latter a corn by-product.

For 1996, Mercury dealers got their own version of the Explorer to sell. Called the Mountaineer, it came with unique trim and a standard V-8.

The 1996 model year would also bring totally redesigned Class 7 and 8 Louisville Line models, closely followed by new Class 8 AeroMax trucks. Ford spent a lot of time, money, and effort developing these vehicles to make them the class of their class, giving them sleek styling intended to take them into the 21st Century. This all proved perplexing a short time later when Ford announced it was seeking to sell off these truck lines, the eventual buyer being archrival Freightliner. Though the sale shocked many observers, it was a move by Ford to free up manufacturing space for its popular light-duty vehicles, such as the Explorer and F-Series pickups.

And speaking of the F-Series, arriving for 1997 was a completely redesigned full-size truck that featured the most-radical changes yet seen from one generation of Ford pickups to the next. Introduced early in the 1996 calendar year, only certain models of the new

F-Series were offered at first, so some versions of the 1996-style trucks continued to be sold alongside them. Among others, these included all the heavy-duty pickups (F-250 HD and F-350), which wouldn't be redesigned until the 1999 model year. Among the F-Series' many early accolades was the coveted Truck of the Year award from *Motor Trend* magazine.

Nineteen ninety-seven also marked the end of the full-size two-door Bronco SUV after a 30-year run. In its place came the even larger four-door Expedition, which was based on the new-for-'97 F-Series, and offered more interior room and more options than Bronco ever did.

Ford Motor Company reached a milestone in 1998 when it celebrated the 50th anniversary of the F-Series brand. And at the smaller end of the truck scale, Ranger received a longer cab and larger standard engine, along with an electric-powered model. The year also brought Lincoln dealers an upscale version of the Expedition called Navigator.

Midway through the '98 model year, Ford finally introduced new heavy-duty F-Series pickups based on the redesigned light-duty versions that had appeared for '97. Tagged as 1999 models, the F-250 HD and F-350 carried a similar but brawnier look, befitting their load-lugging status. Also arriving as a 1999 model was a revised Windstar minivan with dual sliding side doors.

With the addition or redesign of several important vehicles and the deletion of its long-standing heavy-duty lines, it can never be said that Ford didn't close out the 20th century with a bang. In combination, these changes helped position the company for the next century—and its second hundred years.

1990

1990: Ranger adds larger 4.0-liter V-6; Aerostar gets the bigger V-6, too, plus standard antilock rear brakes and an all-wheel-drive version; Econoline also adds standard antilock rear brakes; C-Series Tilt Cab bows out

1-2. Aerostar added all-wheel-drive versions of both passenger and cargo models for 1990. Also added was an available 160-horsepower 4.0-liter V-6 that could be chosen in place of the standard 145-hp 3.0 V-6. Antilock rear brakes were newly standard. 3. Antilock rear brakes were also made standard on the Econoline and Club Wagon. Deleted was the rarely ordered five-speed manual transmission. 4. Newly optional on the Ranger was the same 4.0-liter V-6 added to the Aerostar's engine roster. Gone for '90 was the sporty GT package. 5. Bronco II was in its swan-song year, and was thus carried over with few changes.

4

5

1990

1. Aside from the four-speed overdrive automatic transmission being offered with all engines for 1990, the Bronco received few changes. 2. Ditto for the F-Series pickups, though 4WD models got standard automatic-locking front hubs. 3. The medium-duty Cargo, introduced for 1986, was originally intended to replaced the C-Series Tilt Cab, but it wasn't until 1990 that it actually did so. 4. After an unprecedented 34 years on the market with very few changes, the C-Series breathed its last in 1990. Its demise was a surprise—and disappointment—to many, as it remained one of the most popular trucks of its type right up to its dying day. In this split photo, the 1990 model is on the left, the original '57 version on the right.

1991

1991: Explorer sport-utility introduced; Ranger adds powertrain choices

1-3. Two-wheel-drive Rangers got an optional 3.0-liter V-6 for 1991 to replace the 2.9-liter offered previously (and still optional on 4×4s), gaining five horsepower in the bargain, to 145. Dress-up option packages included the STX (1) and Sport (2). The optional 4.0-liter V-6 could now be linked to a five-speed manual in addition to a four-speed automatic. Regular and SuperCab (3) body styles remained available. 4. Econoline lost its short-wheelbase version for 1991, leaving long-wheelbase models in regular and extended lengths. 5. The Aerostar minivan was the unlikely recipient of a new Sport Appearance Package for '91 that included a front spoiler and side skirts. But the really big news that year was...

1991

Introduced in the spring of 1990 as a '91 model, the Explorer looked quite similar to the Bronco II it replaced. But while the Bronco II came only in a two-door version, the Explorer was offered with either two or four doors. Both were significantly larger than the Bronco II; the two-door by more than a foot, the four-door by nearly two feet. The only engine offered was the Ranger's 155-horsepower 4.0-liter V-6, which helped provide a 5500-lb towing capacity.

Ford's Phenomenal Explorer..................

A colossal hit right out of the box, Ford's Explorer sport-utility vehicle would go on to become one of the company's most important products. It came in two- and four-door body styles (the four-door proving far more popular), and both versions were somewhat larger than their direct competitors. Explorer's combination of passenger and cargo room, maneuverable size, adequate power, and features for the money—along with overwhelmingly favorable magazine reviews—made it America's best-selling SUV in its very first model year on the market. And it has continued to hold that title every year since.

EXPLORER
19M249

1991

New for '91 F-150s was a Nite trim package that included blackout exterior trim and alloy wheels with white-lettered tires. It was offered on both regular and SuperCab models.

1. An optional bed-mounted light bar, rear tube bumper, and side stripes could give the F-150 an off-road flavor. 2-3. A couple of different two-tone paint schemes were available for 1991 on both regular and SuperCab models.

1991

1. An F-800 hosts a "cherry picker," frequently used by telephone repair crews. While many trucks of this size used a diesel engine (which would make it an F-8000), the badge on the grille indicates this unit is powered by the 429-cubic-inch four-barrel V-8 gas engine. 2. Ford's LTL-9000 looked quite dressy when equipped with an aerodynamic sleeper cab, tape stripes, and chrome accessories.

1992

1992: Econoline redesigned; F-Series/Bronco facelifted; Aerostar gets driver-side airbag

1. Ranger's STX package came with side graphics, as shown on this SuperCab 4×4. 2. Sport models got their own distinct—and colorful—graphics. 3. Redesigned for the first time since 1975, the big Econoline vans grew even bigger for 1992. As before, both regular- and extended-length bodies were offered on the same 138-inch wheelbase. Econolines also became the first full-size van to offer a driver-side airbag. 4. Fitted with a raised roof and side lift, the cavernous Econoline was readily adaptable for wheelchair use. 5. Explorer received few changes in its sophomore year. A clone of the two-door version shown was marketed by Ford-owned Mazda as the Navajo.

1-2. F-Series pickups were treated to a front-end restyle for 1992 that resulted in a smoother face. Also for '92, the Flareside bed returned as an option after a four-year absence. It was available on both regular- and extended-cab models. 3. The full-size Bronco received the same new front-end treatment as the F-Series, and also added a Nite trim package similar to that introduced on F-Series the previous year. 4. Ford executives surround one of the company's sleek new AeroMax 120 models that had been introduced for 1991. All featured a set-back front axle along with the most aerodynamic styling ever seen on a heavy-duty Ford truck.

1993

1

1993: Ranger restyled; high-performance F-150 Lightning introduced; Explorer gets four-wheel antilock brakes

2

3

1. Based on Ford of Europe's Escort Van, the Ecostar was an experimental electric vehicle that was not sold to the general public in the U.S., but did see limited fleet use. It was claimed to have a top speed of 75 mph and range of 100 miles courtesy of its sodium-sulfur battery pack. 2-3. A rounded-edge restyle was applied to the Ranger for 1993, its first since '89. A revised interior came along for the ride, but powertrains carried over.

1. Replacing the F-150's Nite package for '93 was the performance-oriented Lightning, which lived up to its name with a special version of the 5.8-liter V-8 packing 240 horsepower, vs. 200 for other 5.8s. Like the Nite, Lightning featured black-out trim, to which was added a sport suspension with 17-inch alloy wheels, front spoiler, and specific bucket seats. 2. New to the Explorer for '93 were four-wheel antilock brakes that replaced a rear-wheel-only system. 3. Ford touted the F-150 Eddie Bauer Expedition as "The outdoorsman's dream vehicle," but never sold it to outdoorsmen—or anyone else. The concept truck featured a bed cover that included a pull-out stove and refrigerator under a protective awning, along with extra storage compartments. What did eventually make it to production was the Expedition name, which would later be applied to a full-size SUV.

3

1994

1994: Four-wheel antilock brakes available on Econoline; F-Series gains driver-side airbag, but drops Lightning

1. Midway through the 1993 model year—in which it was redesigned—Ranger added a sporty Splash model to its lineup that included a Flareside bed and special trim. At first offered only as a regular cab, an extended-cab version was added for 1994. Ford-owned Mazda now sold its own version of the Ranger as the B-Series, but it didn't offer a Flareside bed. 2-3. Full-size vans got four-wheel antilock brakes for 1994. They were optional on Econoline "work" vans (2), standard on Club Wagon passenger vans (3).

1. Ford's high-performance Lightning was dropped from the F-150 lineup for 1994. But an F-150 Flareside could still be ordered with a 5.8-liter V-8; while the Lightning's 240-horsepower version was gone, the remaining 5.8 gained 10 hp for a total of 210. 2. Light-duty F-Series pickups got a driver-side airbag for 1994, but there were few other changes of note.

1995

1995: Windstar minivan introduced; Ranger offers driver-side airbag and four-wheel antilock brakes; Explorer gets facelift along with dual airbags; F-150 Lightning returns

1. Ranger received a host of changes for 1995, including an available driver-side airbag and four-wheel antilock brakes. Also, the grille was revised and the base 2.3-liter four-cylinder engine gained 14 horsepower, now 112. 2. An all-new front-wheel-drive Windstar minivan arrived for 1995 with V-6 engines of 3.0 and 3.8 liters. It was intended to replace the rear/all-wheel-drive Aerostar, but the latter remained popular enough that the two were sold side-by-side for a few years. 3. Explorer received its first styling change since being introduced as a 1991 model. A new grille (in either chrome or body color, depending on trim level) highlighted a rounded front end, and a revised interior included dual front airbags. Both two-door and four-door versions continued to be offered, but the latter remained far more popular. 4. Ford's full-size Bronco sport-utility received only minor trim changes for 1995.

1995

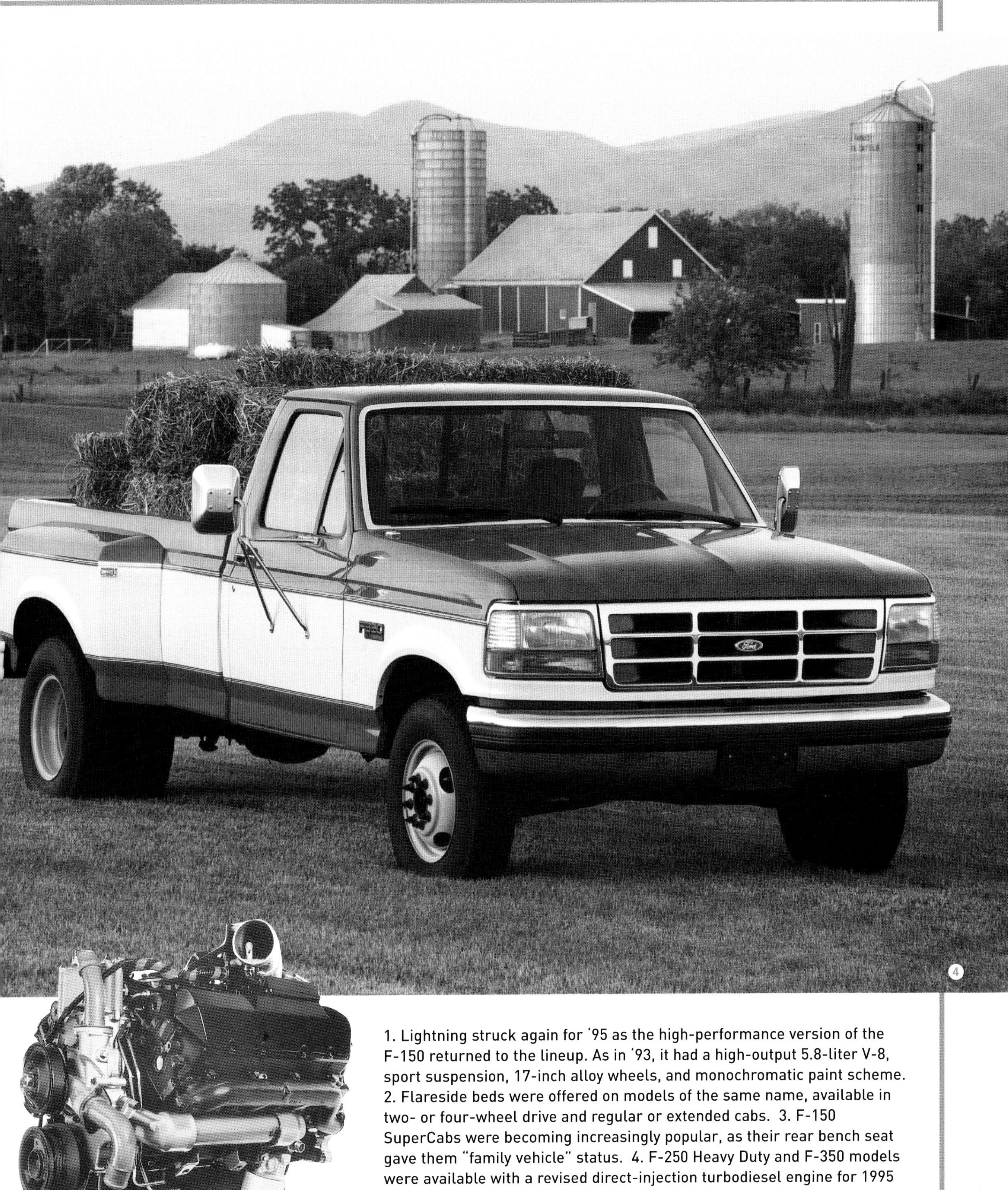

1. Lightning struck again for '95 as the high-performance version of the F-150 returned to the lineup. As in '93, it had a high-output 5.8-liter V-8, sport suspension, 17-inch alloy wheels, and monochromatic paint scheme. 2. Flareside beds were offered on models of the same name, available in two- or four-wheel drive and regular or extended cabs. 3. F-150 SuperCabs were becoming increasingly popular, as their rear bench seat gave them "family vehicle" status. 4. F-250 Heavy Duty and F-350 models were available with a revised direct-injection turbodiesel engine for 1995 (inset) that produced 210 horsepower and a whopping 425 pound-feet of torque—both up significantly over previous versions. The turbodiesel was also offered in heavy-duty versions of the Econoline/Club Wagon.

1996

1996: F-150 Lightning dropped; Explorer adds optional V-8, all-wheel drive, and Mercury Mountaineer clone; Ranger gets dual airbags; AeroMax and Louisville Line of heavy-duty trucks redesigned

1. Rangers added an optional passenger-side airbag for 1996. Included was a switch that allowed the bag to be deactivated if a child seat was placed in the front seat. 2. The aging Aerostar minivan—still offered in rear- or all-wheel-drive versions—continued to attract buyers, even while standing in the shadow of the more modern front-drive Windstar. 3. The full-size Club Wagon passenger van and its cargo-carrying Econoline mate saw few changes for 1996. 4. The 1996 model year would prove the last for the Bronco, as it came to the end of its rope after a 30-year run. Sales of two-door SUVs in general were on the wane, as customers increasingly preferred the convenience of four doors. 5. F-Series pickups continued with few changes for 1996, though dropped from the line were a couple of versions that would overlap with the early arriving (and redesigned) 1997 models, along with the high-performance F-150 Lightning. 6. The heaviest-duty F-Series models got a new look for 1995, with a large square grille and rounded front fenders. A little-changed '96 model is shown. 7. The Louisville Line was redesigned for 1996, getting a sloped windshield and rounded front contours, the latter made more prominent on this version thanks to its set-back front axle.

1996

1. Featuring a laid-back windshield and rounded edges that presented a slippery face to the wind, the AeroMax 9500 was introduced for 1996 as Ford's top truck. 2. Still sold alongside the AeroMax 9500 that year was the blockier AeroMax 120, which had been introduced in 1991. 3. The redesigned Louisville Line included models without a set-back front axle, which made for a flatter front end.

1997

1997: Redesigned F-Series introduced midway through 1996 model year; F-Series-based four-door Expedition replaces the two-door Bronco, which is discontinued; new overhead-cam truck engines debut

1-2. Added to the Explorer's powertrain roster for 1997 was a 205-horsepower 4.0-liter overhead-cam V-6 and five-speed automatic transmission. Still offered was the previous 160-hp 4.0-liter overhead-valve V-6—now also mated to the new five-speed automatic—plus the 210-hp 5.0-liter overhead-valve V-8 with four-speed automatic. Starting in 1996, sister division Mercury began selling a near clone of the Explorer as the Mountaineer. 3. Ranger didn't share the Explorer's new overhead-cam V-6, but did offer the new five-speed automatic transmission.

1997

1-3. In its most radical change since 1980, the F-Series was redesigned for 1997. At first offered only in F-150 form—and even then with a limited lineup—it arrived early in the 1996 calendar year and was sold alongside the '96 models. Both Flareside (1) and Styleside (2) beds were available. Early production focused on SuperCab (extended cab) versions, which featured a rear-hinged back door on the passenger side. These were sometimes called "half doors," as they were smaller than conventional ones. Also, they hinged at the rear and could only be opened after the corresponding front door was opened. 4-6. As production ramped up, regular-cab versions of the F-150 became more plentiful. Grilles came in either body color (4) or chrome (6) depending on trim level. Power came from a trio of new engines: a 4.2-liter overhead-valve V-6, and overhead cam V-8s of 4.6 and 5.4 liters. All produced more horsepower than the larger engines they replaced.
7. Ford didn't waste any time entering the sleek new F-150 in the NASCAR Craftsman Truck Series.

4

5

Raybestos
98
Raybestos BRAKES
Red Carpet Lease
GOODYEAR
F-150
7

6

1997

1-3. For 1997, Econolines and Club Wagons could be ordered with a new overhead-cam V-10 engine based on the new ohc "Modular" V-8s from the F-Series pickups. They also got a passenger-side airbag and restyled grille. 4-5. Effectively replacing the two-door Bronco as Ford's full-size SUV was the four-door Expedition, which was based on the new F-Series pickups. It shared the F-Series' new overhead-cam 4.6- and 5.4-liter V-8s. Dual front airbags and antilock brakes were standard, and a third-row seat that allowed for nine-passenger capacity was optional.

3

4

5

1997

1. The AeroMax 9500 became Ford's top-of-the-line truck when introduced for 1996; a little-changed '97 model is shown. Its aerodynamic front end incorporated flush-mounted wraparound headlights and vertical "nostrils" flanking the upper half of the grille. 2. The slightly smaller Louisville Line used the same cab, hood, and front-fender design, but with different styling features.

1998

1998: Ford celebrates Golden Anniversary of F-Series; Ranger gets longer cab, larger standard engine, and electric version; Windstar adds wider driver's door; Lincoln adds Expedition-based Navigator; Aerostar discontinued; Ford sells heavy-duty truck lines to Freightliner

1

1. Ford introduced the Ranger EV (Electric Vehicle) for 1998. Powered by a rear-mounted 90-horsepower electric motor, the EV claimed a top speed of 75 mph and a range of from 35 to 50 miles from conventional lead-acid batteries mounted between the frame rails. Antilock brakes, dual airbags, and an electric heater were standard; air conditioning was optional. Shared with standard Rangers was a regular cab that was three inches longer than before, allowing for more legroom. 2. The EV's instrument panel included a "Distance to Empty" gauge indicating how far the truck could be driven based on the amount of charge left in the batteries. The "E" on the gear indicator stood for "Economy Drive"; when selected, it increased the amount of electrical regeneration when braking. 3. Not available in EV form was the extended SuperCab, which for 1998 offered dual rear-hinged back doors, a feature not available on any other contemporary compact pickup. Also for '98, Ranger's base engine grew from 2.3 liters to 2.5.

The NASCAR F-150 marked the Golden Anniversaries of both the stock-car racing association and Ford's F-Series pickups. The dual side exhausts shown on this prototype were moved to the rear on production versions.

1998

Ford didn't let the 50th Anniversary of the F-Series pass unnoticed, with numerous promotions depicting the inaugural 1948 version beside (or in some cases, beneath) a new '98 model. In another celebratory gesture, 50 new F-150s were arranged in the corporate oval to be photographed from above.

1998

1. Expedition changed little for its sophomore year—and didn't need to; it had already surpassed every other class competitor in sales. 2. Explorer also saw few changes—and likewise, didn't need any. It remained the best-selling SUV in the country for 1998. 3. Having fallen behind in the sliding side-door game, Windstar sought to combat rivals' new driver-side sliding doors with a wider front passenger door—a helpful six inches wider—that allowed easier access to the rear seats. These 1998 models were released in the spring of 1997, and also wore a revised grille.

1. In a move that surprised—and dismayed—many, Ford elected to sell off its heavy-duty truck lines to Freightliner in the late 1990s. Soon to carry Freightliner's new Sterling badge (a stylized "S" in a surrounding oval) was Ford's top-line Class 8 AeroMax 9500. 2. Shown is one of the last of the Ford-built Louisville Line trucks, versions of which would also later be badged as Sterlings.

1999

1999: More power for Expedition; side airbags for Explorer; dual sliding side doors for Windstar; dual rear doors for F-150; a redesign for F-250 HD and F-350

1

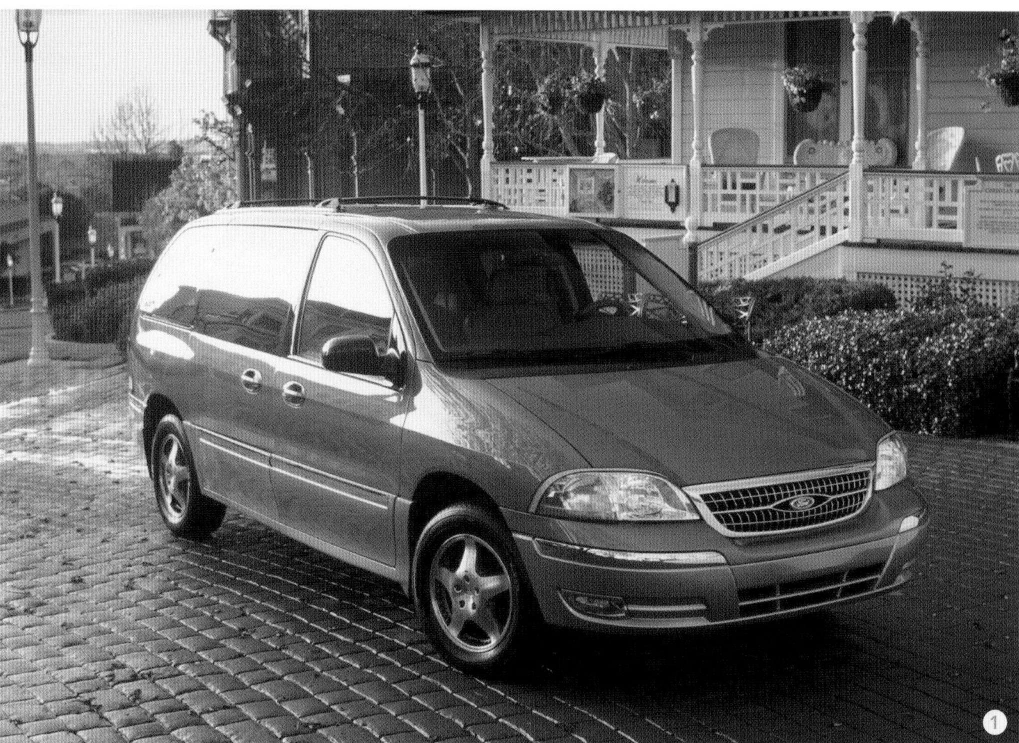

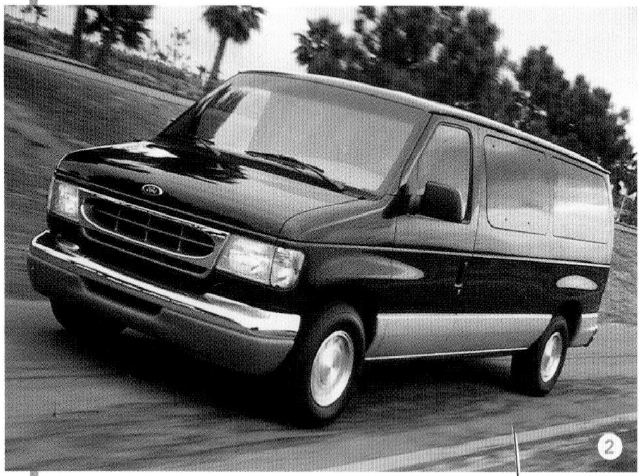

2

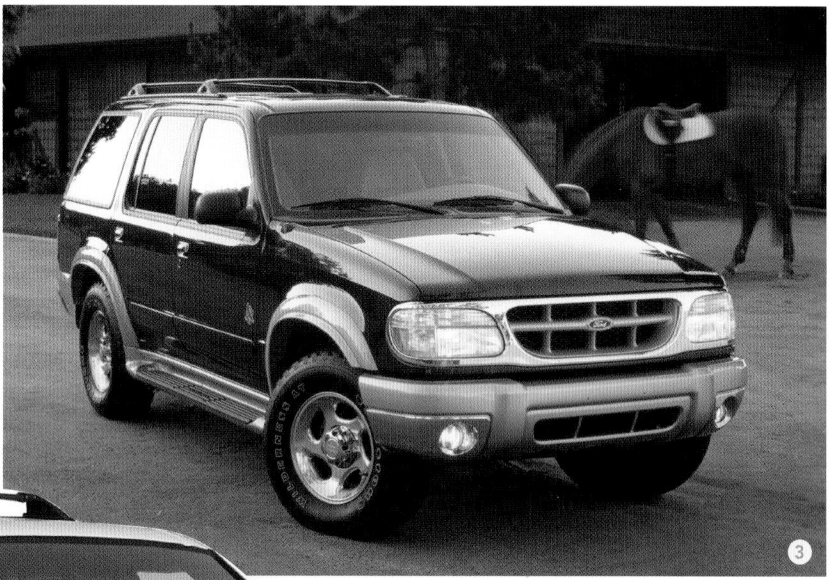

3

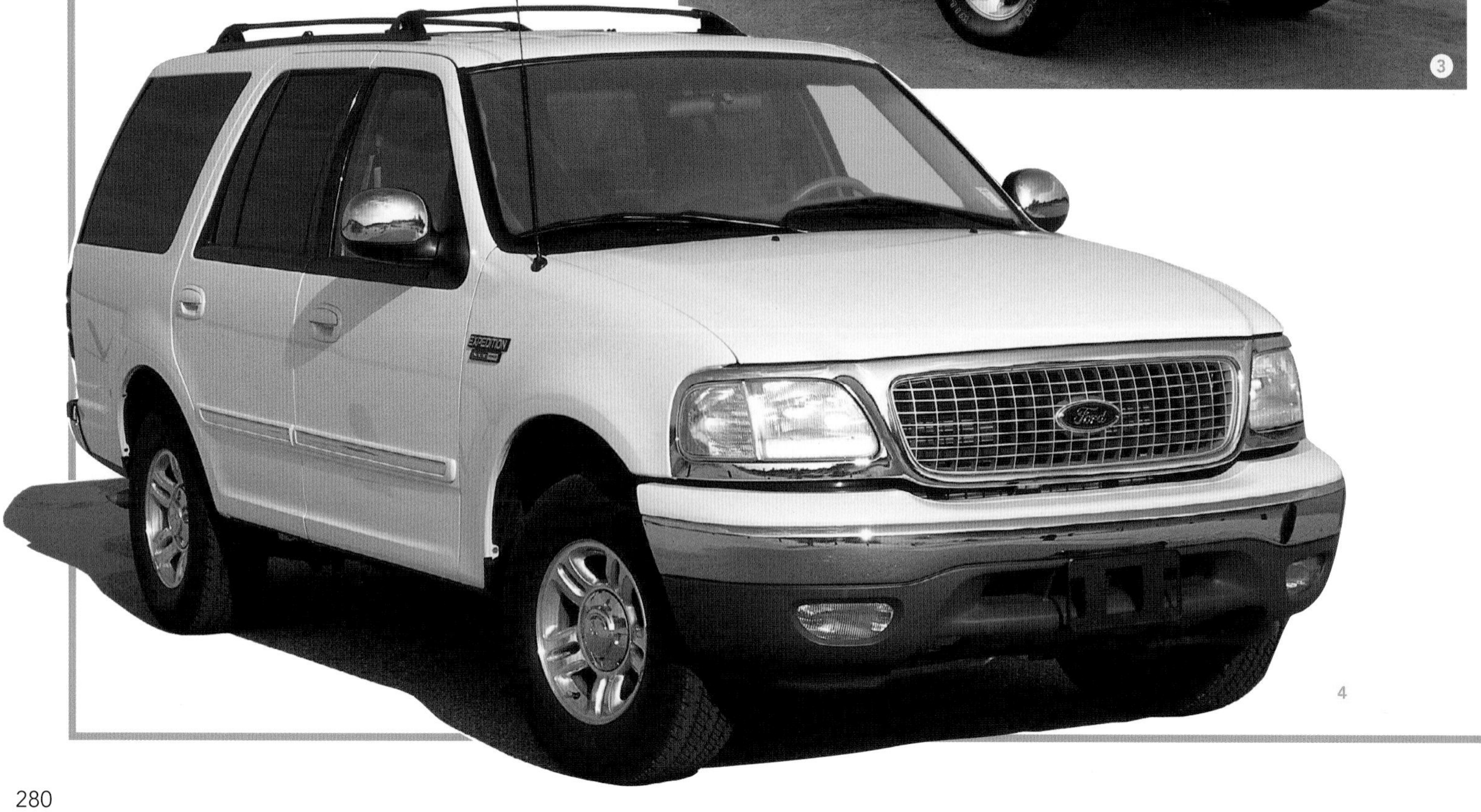

4

5

6

7

1. Windstar joined minivan rivals by adding an available driver-side sliding door for 1999. Other changes included a revised grille and newly optional side airbags. 2. The passenger version of Ford's full-size van changed its name from Club Wagon to Econoline Wagon for 1999, more closely aligning it with its cargo-carrying sibling, the Econoline Van. 3. Front side airbags were newly optional on Explorer. 4. Both of Expedition's available V-8 engines gained power for '99: The 4.6-liter was up by 25 horsepower to 240, the 5.4 gained 30 hp to 260. The grille was restyled, too, and adjustable pedals—which could power fore and aft about three inches—were newly optional. 5. Returning after a three-year hiatus was the high-performance Lightning, and it returned with a vengeance. Again based on the F-150, it now carried an exclusive supercharged version of the 5.4-liter V-8 packing a mighty 360 horsepower. As before, a lowered sport suspension and special trim was included in the package. 6. New for SuperCab versions of the F-150 were dual rear doors; previously, only the passenger side had a rear door. Other changes for '99 included a revised grille and 25 more horsepower for the available 5.4-liter V-8, now with 260. 7. F-250 Heavy Duty and F-350 had lost out when the lighter-duty F-Series models were redesigned for 1997, but made up for it with a redesign of their own for '99. Now called Super Duty, they arrived early in the 1998 calendar year, and like their lighter-duty linemates, offered a SuperCab with dual rear-hinged back doors. Styling touches included grilles incorporating vertical "nostrils" at each edge.

1999

1. Super Duty F-250 HD and F-350 were available in crew cab form with four conventional side doors. Engine choices ranged up to a 6.8-liter V-10 with 275 horsepower, and a 7.3-liter V-8 turbodiesel with 235 hp and a stump-pulling 500 pound-feet of torque. 2. The Super Duty line included even heavier-duty F-450 and F-550 models that could be fitted with a variety of bed styles. 3. After Ford sold the tooling for its big AeroMax and Louisville models to Freightliner, the F-750 took its place as the company's biggest truck.

Chapter Ten: 2000-2006

Improving the Breed and Expanding the Lineup

Ford began the 21st century by releasing a new super-sized sport-utility vehicle bigger than anything else on the market—or that had ever *been* on the market. Called the Excursion, it rode the Super Duty truck chassis that also hosted Ford's F-250 HD pickups. This maximum-duty behemoth dwarfed its closest rival, the Chevrolet Suburban, by being longer, wider, taller, and nearly a ton heavier. Over the years it took some gaff for its poor fuel economy, but with gas prices relatively low at its introduction, buyers were attracted to its cavernous interior and high towing limits.

Also for 2000, Ford joined forces with Harley-Davidson to produce a special-edition F-150 pickup truck called—appropriately—the Harley-Davidson F-150. This marriage of two icons was a marketer's dream come true, as it had crossover appeal to both pickup and motorcycle enthusiasts. The Harley-Davidson F-150 came only as a SuperCab with Flareside bed, and featured distinct interior trim, special wheels and grille, and unique Harley-Davidson badging. It was offered in any color the customer wanted—as long as the customer wanted black.

2000-2006

Chapter Ten

The following model year was another big one for Ford truck enthusiasts. Balancing the huge Excursion SUV introduced for 2000 was the compact Escape, which came with either an economical four-cylinder engine or powerful V-6. Also arriving for 2001 was a version of the Explorer with a short open bed in back rather than an enclosed cargo area. Called the Sport Trac, it was essentially a crew-cab pickup, but offered better interior accommodations than most compact rivals.

Speaking of crew cabs, the F-150 also gained a version for 2001. Called the SuperCrew, it marked the first time a full-size ½-ton pickup was available with four full-size doors. Previously, crew cabs were only available on ¾-ton-and-up trucks. So popular was this body style that the Harley-Davidson F-150 became a SuperCrew for 2001.

Also for 2001, a more powerful engine was offered on Explorer and Ranger, and the Ranger gained a sporty version called the Edge. And buyers wanting to tow large fifth-wheel trailers in style were offered a decked-out four-door F-650 model called the Super CrewZer.

For 2002, the Explorer received a complete redesign, the first since its introduction eleven years earlier. New were a third-row seating option and standard independent rear suspension. Also that year, the Harley-Davidson F-150 got a horsepower boost courtesy of a supercharger for its 5.4-liter V-8, and for the first time was available in grey as well as black.

The biggest news for 2003 was not a product, but rather a celebration—that of Ford's 100th anniversary. An event held in the company's hometown of Dearborn, Michigan, attracted thousands of Ford fans eager to join in the festivities. To commemorate the anniversary, Ford introduced special Heritage Edition F-150s with two-tone paint and interior treatment, along with "1903-2003" Heritage Edition badges. Other specially trimmed pickups offered that year were the Harley-Davidson F-150 with "100th Anniversary Edition" badges and available black-over-silver paint, and the King Ranch F-150 with rich leather upholstery and other unique features. Also for 2003, Expedition earned a redesign, gaining independent rear suspension and the industry's first power-folding third-row seat.

Two different styles of F-150 pickups were offered by Ford for the 2004 model year. The first was a selection of carryover 2003 models in regular-cab and SuperCab form called F-150 Heritage. The other was a completely redesigned truck with new styling inside and out, as well as a new chassis. Regular-cab versions gained narrow, rear-hinged "quarter doors" in back that were similar to the SuperCab's "half doors," and allowed easy access to the cargo area behind the front seats. Only the new version offered a SuperCrew body with four conventional doors. The Heritage disappeared after 2004, presumably kept in the lineup only until production could be ramped up on the new version.

The Harley-Davidson edition returned for 2004, but instead of being based on the F-150, it appeared in the F-250 Super Duty line. It was offered in SuperCab or SuperCrew form, with four-wheel drive, a choice of 6.8-liter V-10 or 6.0-liter V-8 turbodiesel power, and a black-and-orange (Harley-Davidson's official colors) paint scheme. Also for 2004, the Windstar minivan was updated and renamed Freestar.

New for 2005 was a gas/electric hybrid version of the Escape compact SUV. Its drivetrain coupled a four-cylinder engine with an electric motor, and the vehicle would run on a combination of the two or on either source alone depending on conditions. Fuel economy was impressive, with EPA ratings (33 city/29 highway) that bested the regular four-cylinder model by a substantial margin.

Also new this year was a car/SUV "crossover" called the Freestyle. Larger than the Escape, less trucklike than the Explorer, it could seat up to seven and featured Ford's first Continuously Variable Transmission (CVT).

Dropped at the end of the 2005 model year was the big Excursion sport-utility vehicle. Its demise coincided with soaring gas prices but wasn't decided by them; the determination to drop it had been made long before, as sales had been sagging for some years.

Since its introduction for 1991, Ford's Explorer had always been the number-one-selling SUV in the United States. To keep it on top, a revised version was introduced for 2006 featuring bolder styling, a redesigned interior, and an updated chassis. A more powerful V-8 was offered, too, mated to a new six-speed automatic transmission.

The Harley-Davidson pickup returned to the F-150 line for 2006, taking the form of a SuperCab with two- or four-wheel drive and a 5.4-liter 300-horsepower V-8. Aside from that, other trucks received only minor changes that year, as Ford was concentrating its efforts on cars.

Though the Ford Motor Company is currently suffering some financial woes, it has faced adversity before and come out stronger than ever. And if the company's activities in the early part of the 21st century are any indication, there's a lot to look forward to in the coming years.

2000

2000: Excursion bows as America's biggest SUV; Windstar adds rear-seat DVD entertainment and other new options; Harley-Davidson F-150 introduced

1-2. Explorer was little changed for 2000, continuing to be offered in four-door form (shown) and as the two-door Explorer Sport. 3. The Windstar minivan added optional power-adjustable pedals and rear-seat DVD entertainment system for 2000. 4. The hot SVT Lightning with its 360-horsepower supercharged V-8 could run the 0-60-mph dash in under six seconds. 5. An agreement with Harley-Davidson Motor Company produced the new-for-2000 F-150 Harley-Davidson pickup. Available only in SuperCab form—and only in black—it was powered by a 260-hp 5.4-liter V-8.

4

5

2000

1-2. The big news—literally—in Ford-trucks for 2000 was the new full-size-plus Excursion. Based on the F-250 HD Super Duty pickup platform, it was advertised as the world's biggest, heaviest sport-utility vehicle. Indeed, its 227-inch length stretched out 22 inches farther than an Expedition's (no small fry itself), and at 7087 lbs., was nearly a ton heavier. Engine choices included a 5.4-liter V-8, 6.8-liter V-10, and a 7.3-liter turbodiesel V-8. 3. As a consolation for no longer being Ford's biggest SUV, the Expedition got optional front side airbags and rear obstacle detection for 2000.

1

2

3

2001

2001: Ford expands its SUV fleet with compact Escape; Explorer line expanded with Sport Trac crew cab; F-150s gain SuperCrew four-door version and four-wheel antilock brakes; Ranger adds sporty Edge models, more V-6 power; Super CrewZer joins Super Duty line

1-2. Ford's biggest truck news for 2001 was the Escape compact SUV. The design was a joint effort with Mazda, Ford's Japanese affiliate, which offered its own version as the Tribute. Escape quickly rose to the top of its class in sales thanks to a winning combination of carlike driving traits, user-friendly utility, and attractively low prices. A lone four-door wagon body style was offered with a choice of four-cylinder or V-6 power, front-wheel drive or optional all-wheel drive, and initially, XLS and uplevel XLT trim. Antilock brakes and front side airbags were among the options. 3. Explorer made few changes for an abbreviated 2001 model year.

2001

1. Pickup or SUV? The Explorer Sport Trac was both. Released in early calendar 2000 as a 2001 model, it combined the Explorer's front end and cabin with a four-foot-long cargo bed. 2. Econoline Wagons offered a Traveler option for 2001 that included leather upholstery, rear-seat DVD entertainment system with dual screens, and two-tone paint. On all Econolines, four-wheel antilock brakes were now standard. 3. William Clay Ford, Jr., great grandson of founder Henry Ford, became CEO of Ford Motor Company in the fall of 2001. As such, he was the first Ford to lead the company since Henry Ford II, who retired in 1980. 4. Sporty Edge models were added to the Ranger line, with two-wheel-drive versions getting the 4×4's taller ride height. Also for 2001, the 4.0-liter V-6 went from an overhead-valve configuration to overhead-cam, gaining 47 horsepower in the bargain, now at 207. 5. With the addition of a new SuperCrew crew-cab body style for 2001, the F-150 became the first ½-ton pickup to offer four conventional side doors. Previously, crew cabs were offered only in ¾-ton-and-up pickups. 6-7. New to the Super Duty line for 2001 was the huge F-650 Super CrewZer, which featured a 300-hp turbodiesel V-8 and luxury interior. 8. The Harley-Davidson F-150 switched to the new four-door SuperCrew body for 2001. Carried over were its 260-hp 5.4-liter V-8, polished 20-inch wheels, and "Any color so long as it's black" palette. 9. The SVT Lightning returned with its 360-hp supercharged 5.4, 18-inch wheels, and Flareside bed. It again came only in regular-cab form.

1

2

3

4

5

6

7

8

9

2002

2002: Redesigned Explorer introduced; Ranger and F-150 add off-road-oriented FX4 models; Supercharged V-8 muscles up third-edition Harley-Davidson F-150 pickup

1

1-2. A redesigned Explorer was introduced as an early 2002 model. It featured a roomier interior, available third-row seating, and class-exclusive independent rear suspension. 3. Ranger added an off-road-ready FX4 four-wheel-drive version for 2002 with heavy-duty springs, 31-inch tires, and heftier skid plates.

2002

An even hotter F-150 Harley-Davidson SuperCrew arrived for 2002 with a potent supercharged version of Ford's 5.4-liter V-8 making a stout 340 horsepower. This third limited-edition F-150 came in the traditional Harley black, but also in a new Dark Shadow Grey, pictured here. Other features included a bright "billet" grille, unique 20-inch chrome wheels, low-riding suspension, and a posh cab with leather upholstery and brushed-metal accents.

2003

2003: Ford Motor Company observes its historic 100th anniversary; updated Expedition debuts

1. Expedition was redesigned for 2003, gaining independent rear suspension and availability of the industry's first power-folding third-row seat. Options included antiskid control and curtain side airbags. 2-3. Top-line King Ranch trim, introduced with the F-150 SuperCrew (shown), was made available for Flareside SuperCab models for 2003. 4. The 2003 Harley-Davidson F-150 SuperCrew wore 100th anniversary badging; as it so happened, both Ford Motor Company and Harley-Davidson celebrated their centennials that year. This striking black-over-silver two-tone paint scheme was optional. Power still came from a supercharged 5.4-liter V-8 making 340 horsepower. 5. The Lightning's supercharged 5.4 V-8 gained 20 hp for a total of 380.

2003

Ford's PR department worked overtime on historically themed press photos to trumpet the company's 2003 centennial. Among them was this pairing of an early Model T touring car with a Super Duty F-250 crew cab pickup, one of the most popular models in Ford's "big rig" line.

2004

2004: F-Series light-duty pickups redesigned; Ford sells some previous F-Series models under the Heritage nameplate; limited-edition Harley-Davidson shifts to the Super Duty line; two-door Explorer Sport dropped; Windstar minivan revamped to become the Freestar

1. Smoother looks rejuvenated Ford's minivan for 2004, prompting a name change from Windstar to Freestar. A version was newly offered through Mercury dealers as the Monterey. Topping the engine lineup was a new 201-horsepower 4.2-liter V-6.
2. Expedition returned from its 2003 makeover with few changes.

Ford heralded the redesigned 2004 F-150 with special signage on its "Glass House" world headquarters in Dearborn, Michigan. As America's best-selling vehicle for more than two decades—not to mention its importance to Ford's finances—the F-Series got special attention in its latest iteration.

2004

1

2

1. The new F-150 was a study in beautiful brawn. The popular four-door SuperCrew (pictured) returned, but all body styles had four doors—even the regular cab, which had two small "quarter doors" in back to ease access to storage space behind the front seat. 2. F-150s were offered in five trim levels for 2004, each with specific styling details. Shown (from left) are the XLT, STX, Lariat, and FX4. 3. Interiors were redesigned with a modern, hi-tech look. 4. The SVT Lightning retained its 2003 styling for '04, as did some models sold as Heritage Editions. 5. This year's Harley-Davidson edition was a 4WD Super Duty F-250 crew cab with standard two-tone paint.

2004

Ford's heavyweight F-650 and F-750 series offered an expanded 2004 lineup with a bewildering array of choices. There were now no fewer than eight basic models spanning three cab styles, 38 wheelbase/cab combinations, three engines, 14 power ratings, 19 transmissions, and eight seating packages. Uplevel models wore a chrome version of the imposing "nostril" grille that made the big-rig Fords hard to miss.

Ford goes "green" with new Escape Hybrid; all-new Freestyle "crossover" SUV debuts

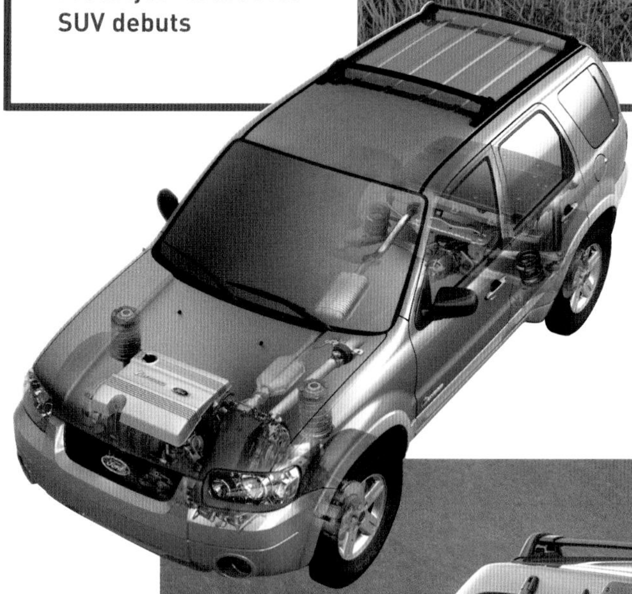

Though delayed by some two years, the 2005 Escape Hybrid was still in time to give Ford the first hybid SUV. A special 2.3-liter gasoline four-cylinder engine and a battery-powered electric motor were combined with a continuously variable automatic transmission. The vehicle could run on either or both power sources, depending on driving needs. The CVT helped optimize the maximum 155 horsepower for performance roughly between that of the regular four-cylinder and V-6 Escapes. Sales were strong from day one.

2005

1

1. Freestyle was Ford's new 2005 entry in the fast-growing market for car-based "crossover" SUVs. Offered with front- or all-wheel drive, all came with a 3.0-liter V-6 and new continuously variable transmission (CVT). Three rows of seats could accommodate up to seven passengers. Front side airbags and curtain side airbags were optional, as were power adjustable pedals, rear-seat DVD entertainment, and rear obstacle detection. 2. The Expedition's standard 5.4-liter V-8 was boosted to 300 horsepower for 2005, up 40 from '04. Top-line Limited models offered heated and cooled front seats.

2

1-2. Econoline vans were spruced up for '05 with a minor facelift and revised dashboard. 3-4. Excursion also got a fresh face for what would turn out to be its swan-song year. Sales of the gargantuan SUV had been sliding in the face of higher gas prices.

2005

1-2. The luxury King Ranch edition returned to the F-150 line for 2005 after a one-year hiatus. 3-4. The high-riding F-150 FX4 models came standard with the 300-horsepower 5.4-liter V-8 that was also available on other F-150s.
5. Like SuperCab models, regular-cab F-150s had two rear "half doors," but they were smaller and used strictly for access to a storage area behind the seats.

1

1. Middleweight F-450 and 550 Super Dutys were restyled for 2005 with Ford's signature "nostril" truck grille. 2. The Super Duty's optional 6.8-liter Triton V-10 went to 355 horsepower for '05, up from 310. Properly equipped, an F-350 pickup (shown) was rated to tow up to 17,000 lbs. 3. The big F-650/F-750 tractors carried a taller but similarly styled grille.

2

3

2006

Explorer gets a major makeover; Ranger gets fresh face; F-Series Harley-Davidson edition revised; Excursion dropped

1-2. Ranger was restyled for 2006 to align it with the corporate"Ford Truck look" and got a more modern dashboard, too. 3. An optional navigation system was the main news for Freestyle. 4. Escapes sported minor cosmetic updates. Ford worked overtime to meet strong demand for the fuel-thrifty Hybrid (shown). 5-6. The versatile Econolines continued to find favor among commercial users ranging from tour operators to general contractors. 7. This year's biggest Econoline Wagons boasted a newly standard antiskid system.

4

5

6

7

2006

1-3. Explorer fended off new competition with a comprehensive 2006 makeover. Among the many changes were a reengineered structure, revised suspension, reworked interior, bold front-end styling, and an available 292-horsepower V-8. 4. With Excursion gone, the Expedition was Ford's largest SUV for 2006. Changes were few. 5. Super Duty pickups with top-line Lariat trim added several formerly optional features. A new Amarillo package dressed the Lariat Crew Cab with Blazing Yellow paint and 18-inch forged-aluminum wheels. 6-8. This year's Harley-Davidson edition reverted to the SuperCab F-150 body and offered a first-time choice of two- or four-wheel drive. The only engine was a 292-hp 5.4-liter V-8, the only color choice a menacing black accented by pinstripes, a "billet" grille, and unique 22-inch wheels.

4

5

6

7

8

2006

1. The 6.0-liter Power Stroke diesel V-8 available in Super Duty pickups was revised for '06 to earn Low Emissions Vehicle (LEV) status, reflecting Ford's commitment to "greener" vehicles of all kinds. Power and torque were unaffected, so workhorses like this F-350 crew cab Stake Bed still had muscle to spare. 2-3. The brawny F-650/F-750 cab/chassis was a solid foundation for all sorts of applications. The choice of regular cab, extended SuperCab, and four-door crew cab was a big plus in the commercial Class 6 and Class 7 truck markets.

1

2

3

LOOK...
LOOK INTO...

INDEX

FORD
Bonus Built
BUILT STRONGER TO LAST
Star-spangled NEW!
Strikingly DIFFERENT!
Excitingly MODERN!

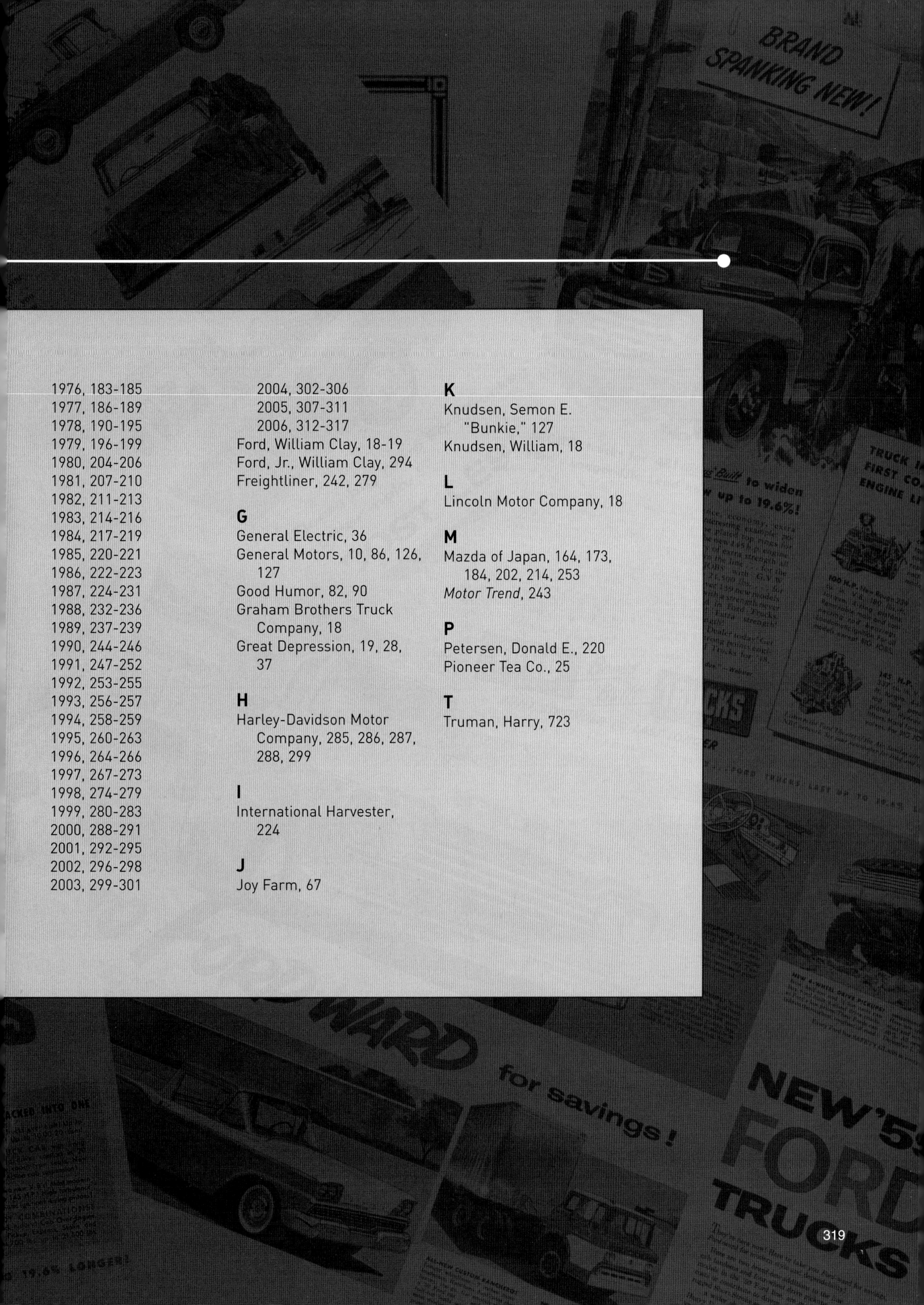